THE SOLDIER'S STORY
THE INVISIBLE WOUNDS FROM WAR

by

JOCEPHUS J. DUCKWORTH

ISBN: 978-1-5356-0336-2

TO: Toni

My book is dedicated to help stop the 22 suicide deaths a day amongst our fellow War Veterans. One suicide death is one to many.

[signature]

11 November 2018

I give thanks to the Lord Jesus Christ to give me the strength to write my stories to save others and help society to understand what we have to endure to fight for America's freedom and understand the aftermath on what we go through once we return home from war.

I give thanks to the Soldiers whom I served with in Iraq January 2003- November 2009 and thanks to all staff members at the Wounded Warrior Transition Battalion at Schofield Barracks, Hawaii. I give thanks to my two good friends in Portland, Oregon, Peggy Porter & Colleen Kerns for helping with the first rough draft editing.

Front Cover Design by Kelli Ann Morgan @ Inspire Creative Services.

Thank you for buying my book. Your purchase will help with awareness about PTSD and help put a stop to the 22 suicide deaths a day amongst our fellow veterans. If you leave a review on Amazon or Barnes and Noble, it will also help get the word out there and be greatly appreciated.

Contents

Introduction

The stories in this book will take you on a journey through the Soldier's eyes. You will see the transformation of the Soldier's character from ordinary E-4 Specialist to war fighting, "get'er done" type of Soldier who has had a difficult time shutting off the combat war mind-set. This Soldier's story will show how six years at war—four tours to Iraq—led to Post-Traumatic Stress Disorder (PTSD) and how he had to fight for three years to get medical treatment from the United States Army. The readers will see and learn the three types of PTSD group sessions the Soldier was involved in and what he has learned from it. The stories will take you on a journey about how difficult it can be when a war Veteran retires from the Army and has a difficult time dealing with civilian life and lack of family structure and support, not to mention jobs.

The book will show how, despite the struggles from war and difficult time adjusting to civilian life, the Soldier never resorted to street drugs or prescription drugs, and never indulged in alcohol. The Soldier's soul was lost, but by God's great mercy, the Soldier found salvation through Jesus Christ.

Soldier still takes it one day at a time to adjust to civilian life and learns how to be Jocephus Duckworth and not Staff Sergeant Duckworth in Iraq.

Prior to 11 September 2001

I arrived at Fort Sill, Oklahoma, around March 2001 to join with Bravo 62nd Engineers. This was my second duty station after coming from Charlie Company 864th Engineers stationed in Fort Wainwright, Alaska. I spent three and a half years in Alaska prior to arriving at Fort Sill, Oklahoma. When I arrived in Fort Sill, the Company's First Sergeant knew me by name because of a few of my battle buddies, with whom I served from Charlie Company. They informed the First Sergeant that I was a good Soldier and very skilled in my Military Occupation Specialist (MOS). I could tell that the 62nd Engineers were a somewhat laid-back unit, compared to Charlie 864th Engineers.

While assigned to Charlie Company for three years, I went on five out of seven deployments, conducting Construction Engineering projects throughout the South Pacific and Alaska. Bravo 62nd Engineers were so laid back that it began to frustrate me. I remember getting a small project as an E-4 that required me to lay over 5,000 square feet of carpet at Building 475. We called this type of a job a "drug deal" because someone on base, mostly high ranking, needed something done immediately. They could cut through all the red tape and just call the First Sergeant to see if he had any skilled Engineer Soldiers to do the job; this was where I came in. I loved it when the First Sergeant found those "drug deals" because it kept me busy and Army life was fun for the moment.

As time went on, however, I wanted to go to school and study heating and air conditioning. I don't know why, but somehow I believed it would be good knowledge to have in the field of Construction Engineering. During this time, I really wondered what to do with myself. The window for reenlistment was approaching and I was getting agitated. I was used to engaging in a mission, like when

I was in Alaska and I had that feeling that I wanted to deploy somewhere to continue working on projects. I kept telling my battle buddy I had this feeling that we would be going to war soon. He asked me how I knew and I said I didn't know, but if you do the math there is always some country that wants to start something with the United States every ten years. Desert Storm kicked off in 1991 and here it was 2001, and I felt that something bad was going to happen.

Attack on 11 September 2001

Early that morning, I got up as normal for physical training (PT) at 0500. I drove less than a fifteen-minute ride to the basic training gate and waited for 0600 PT formation. For sixty minutes, PT was conducted as normal and then I drove back to my home on North West Williams Street.

After showering and eating breakfast, I was in the bedroom shining my boots and listening to the news in the living room. Then I heard the unspeakable words that the first plane had flown into one of the Twin Towers. My first thought was, *Man, is it that cloudy or foggy that the plane had to hit the building?* At this point, I never gave it any thought that the United States was under attack. In order to properly define an attack on American soil, I would refer back to the attack on Pearl Harbor. I truly thought the first hit was a pure accident because there was a time when planes were falling out of the sky due to mechanical problems. When the second plane hit the towers, I knew then it was not an accident. My next question was, *Who did this and why?* The third plane hit the Pentagon and by then I started to wonder if the White House was next. I was late leaving my house, but after what I'd just seen I knew it had affected America and its way of life forever. I mean every American across the United States was affected by this tragedy.

When I left the house there was a high volume of traffic on my street and I thought, *What the hell is going on?* I finally got out of my neighborhood and on to Sheridan Boulevard headed toward Sheridan Gate, which was three minutes from the house. When I got to the corner of Smith and Sheridan, the line was extremely backed up. In fact, there was a city police officer directing traffic. Instead of making the right turn from Smith Boulevard onto Sheridan, the police officer was making all the traffic from Smith turn left to get to the end of the line if you were trying to get on Fort Sill Army Base. Since I didn't have a choice, I went down as far as Lee Blvd (about four miles) to get at the end of the line. The reason why the line was super long to get on base was because everything went on high alert, which meant that security force was checking every square inch of each vehicle for weapons and other explosive devices. As I was only four miles from post, I was in line for three hours and had only moved less than a mile; some vehicles were overheating while idling. Some businesses tried to boost their business by coming out to the long line of cars to sell food and drinks. Four hours later, I finally came to my senses and realized I wouldn't be able to get on base, so I ended up heading home with some crazy maneuvering to get to my house, which was less than a mile away.

For about five days, it was the same situation trying to get on base. Back then, most of us didn't have cell phones, so I stayed home waiting for the house phone to ring for further instructions from my Squad Leader.

During those five days, my eyes were glued to the television wondering who attacked United States and why. I thought, *Who in the hell has the fucking balls to mess with the United States?* The way I saw it at that time was whoever started a fight against the United States had just awakened the giant, and they should know that the US would bring a fight! When I found out it was Osama bin Laden from Afghanistan, three things came to mind: Who is he? Why is he fucking with us? And where in the hell is Afghanistan? This was the part where I wish I had paid attention in history class back in high school. I knew some of the bad guys like Saddam Hussein, who kept quiet for a long time after Desert Storm, and Muammar Gaddafi, but I hadn't heard anything about him since the sixth grade. Then we had Manuel Noriega, but United States ended his career back in 1989. Osama bin Laden—I didn't have a clue about who he was and why he was fucking with us. Once I found out where in the hell Afghanistan was located on the map and saw what the terrain looked like in that area, I knew it going to be a very tough job finding his ass.

Things had gotten better as far as getting on base, but it was extremely hectic when it came to military training. Military training was ten times more intense than basic training. At this point, Bravo Company never received orders about going to Afghanistan, but there was nothing wrong with being proactive.

I remember spending months training putting on our nuclear, biological, and chemical protection face masks (NBC mask) in under nine seconds. Physical training (PT) was more intense than normal; I think we conducted a PT test every other month until it was time to deploy. We spent countless days at the M16 weapon range. I liked this training the most because you can't be a Soldier in the United States Army and not know how to shoot. There's a reason why there's the old saying "one shot, one kill," which is mainly a sniper motto. I remember a Soldier who couldn't shoot to save his life, and I often wondered how he made it through basic training. He spent month after month at the range piggybacking with other units, but he never qualified. I remember throughout the unit's training, the chain of command talked about kicking the Soldier out of the Army. I realized that the chain of command wasn't playing, the United States Army was serious about all military training, and this was the time to weed out the weak and keep the strong to win battles.

On 22 June 2002, I reenlisted for four years in the Army, and I did this because American lives were turned upside down and American freedom was in jeopardy. Also, I wanted to be part of an organized team that won battles that led to winning wars. Not to mention, I wanted to go to war and represent the family name so that my mom and dad could hold their heads up high knowing their son was doing his job well for the American people.

During this time, we trained heavy on our vehicles, keeping up on maintenance and how to report maintenance problems. I didn't find out how important vehicle maintenance was until we deployed to the Middle East. Let's just say you didn't want to be that guy whose vehicle broke down on the roads somewhere in the Middle East.

We also conducted training on 9 Line Medevac. 9 Line Medevac is the most important training you need to know in the battlefields; in the civilian world it is just like dialing 911, but much more detailed. We trained on 9 Line Medevac using sin guard's radio to communicate to the dispatcher.

When a Soldier or Soldiers are wounded in the battlefield, you need the first five lines to get the bird in the air (Medevac chopper). The first five lines are:

Line 1. Location of the pickup site.

Line 2. Radio frequency, call sign, and suffix.

Line 3. Number of patients by precedence:
A - Urgent
B - Urgent Surgical
C - Priority
D - Routine
E - Convenience

Line 4. Special equipment required:
A - None
B - Hoist
C - Extraction Equipment
D - Ventilator

Line 5. Number of patients:
A - Litter
B - Ambulatory

As you can see, you need to know the first five lines to get the bird in the air under stressful conditions. The remaining four are:

Line 6. Security at pickup site:
N - No enemy troops in area

P - Possible enemy troops in area (approach with caution)
E - Enemy troops in area (approach with caution)
X - Enemy troops in area (armed escort required)
* In peacetime—number and types of wounds, injuries, and illnesses

Line 7. Method of marking pickup site:
A - Panels
B - Pyrotechnic Signal
C - Smoke Signal
D - None
E - Other

Line 8. Patient nationality and status:
A - US Military
B - US Civilian
C - Non-US Military
D - Non-US Civilian
E - EPW (Enemy Prisoner of War)

Line 9. NBC Contamination:
N - Nuclear
B - Biological
C - Chemical
* In peacetime—terrain description of pickup site

For each number (1–9) you have to pick what letter fits the situation you're in. For example, line 6 if the situation is E, I would report line 6 (Eco), so line 7 would report line 7 (Alfa), and that would be how 9 Line Medevac was carried out in the battlefield. We trained time after time after time because when your battle buddy is wounded, his or her life is on the line, life is slipping away by the second, and that's why you have to be Johnny-on-the-spot with the 9 Line Medevac.

Around October 2002, the unit received orders to deploy. We, as Soldiers in the unit, assumed Afghanistan, but we didn't know where in Afghanistan. Most of us didn't know a damn thing about Afghanistan other than tough terrain and high elevation. The other thing we didn't know was when we were leaving. Most of us thought we would miss Thanksgiving and Christmas. Times like these were frustrating with Soldiers and their families. It was almost like a G14 classified mission (like the funny line in *Rush Hour*) that was top secret. We were lucky to enjoy a good Thanksgiving and Christmas with family and friends. For me, being with family and friends for the holidays was like having the Last Supper with Jesus Christ. For the next thirteen years, Thanksgiving and Christmas would never been the same for me.

January 2003

Around mid-January, it was on like Donkey Kong. At zero dark thirty at the motor pool, it was 100 percent full accountability. We still didn't know where in the hell we were deploying. Around two o'clock in the morning, the whole company was on lock down ready to be airlifted. For the first time, we finally got the briefing that we were all waiting to hear. Our jaws dropped when we found out we weren't going to Afghanistan; we were deploying to Iraq. It was a shocker because the fight was in Afghanistan. We all wondered why we were heading to Iraq. We all knew that Saddam's army had their asses handed to them back in Desert Storm, but as all Soldiers know, we had to follow orders. Our mission was to construct a petroleum distribution system, which would be essential for coalition success in their invasion of Iraq. For a mission this critical, the war in Iraq seemed much bigger than the war in Afghanistan, and my only question was why? My best bet was that it had a lot to do with some political game that our government wanted to play that cost many Soldiers and Marines their lives. I had a feeling that the pipeline mission and being in a war-type situation would put us to the test to see who we really were as individuals and to see how we worked as team players under extreme stress.

The Pipeline Mission

With my first experience in war with the United States Army, I learned that most combat missions could not get done without the assets of Construction Engineers. There's a reason there's the motto: "Engineers Lead the Way." Most Army branches are categorized as being operations' support: maneuver, fires, effects, and/or force sustainment, but engineers have mission sets within each of these categories, particularly in areas such as mobility assurance and construction. Operations Support Engineers advise the Maneuver Commanders on the effective use of terrain, construction efforts, and the improvement and maintenance of routes, bridges, and airfields. The pipeline constructed to support Operation Iraqi Freedom is the longest operational inland petroleum distribution system (IPDS) tactical fuel pipeline the Army has ever constructed.

- 1,500 Soldiers were required to build and operate IPDS.
- Army Engineer Soldiers hand laid and coupled in excess of 66,000 pipe sections (220 miles) and constructed 20 pump stations.
- Engineer Soldiers manhandled more than 4,500 tons of pipe material (each pipe was 6 inches in diameter, 19 feet long, and 120 pounds.)
- Approximately 35 million gallons of fuel were used in March 2003.
- IPDS was essential in supplying fuel to air and ground forces in Operation Iraqi Freedom.

Battles could not be won without the outstanding efforts of all the Soldiers who built and operated inland petroleum distribution systems. In my opinion, Engineer Soldiers are a great contribution toward winning wars.

Events that Accrued
During Wartime Missions

In March 2003, at Camp Udairi in Kuwait, when the first rounds of fire went off with the Patriot missiles firing toward Baghdad, we were all in Mission-Oriented Protective Posture (MOP 4) gear for about thirty-six hours. We had little to no sleep, sitting in just basic army-issued tents with no hard shell cover.

In April 2003, the Bravo Company 62nd Engineer Battalion laid pipeline for fuel (220 miles) in the desert. A situation accrued wherein an eighteen-wheeler truck came out of nowhere and sped toward us as we were laying pipe. One of the Soldiers yelled out saying there was a truck coming toward us, but by then the Lieutenant (LT) grabbed his weapon and tried to flag the truck down to stop at a safe distance. The truck driver came so close to our Platoon I could look through my iron sights with my 249 Squad Automatic Weapon (SAW), which was sitting on top of the hood of our Humvee. I looked at the driver straight in his eyes and all the other Soldiers followed suit to draw their weapons and aim them at the truck driver. The LT yelled at the truck driver in Arabic, telling him to turn around and go back. It was a five-minute standoff between the truck driver and us. But if the LT would have fired the first shot, I was going to follow suit with my 249 weapon that fired eighty-five rounds a minute with a basic load of one thousand rounds.

Life on the pipeline mission was very tough, but I stayed motivated throughout the seven months that we laid pipeline for fuel. We didn't have the normal camp that Soldiers would have today, like fast food, ice cream shops, or the PX. We had to make our own camps, so we would make camp twenty miles ahead of the pipeline, which meant every week we moved camp. During our camp we would have a small chow tent or trailer, and we would eat whatever the cooks made that day, which was mostly dinner chow. For me, I missed a lot of dinner chow due to the fact that when working twelve to fifteen hours laying pipe, I was so tired that I just stayed in the back of the truck and slept. I had some small snacks from care packages that my family sent, like homemade Rice Krispy treats, cookies, Tang powder orange juice, and crackers or Wheat Thins. I also brought thirty-five dollars' worth of Gatorade from Camp Udairi, so at night I would have Gatorade and some snacks for dinner in the back of the truck. During lunch we would eat the Meals Ready to Eat (MRE). For me, I would eat one item a day out of the MRE bag, so if it was a bag of M&Ms, I would eat that until the next meal break, eight to twelve hours later. The reason for that was because it was too damn hot to eat a full meal, and if I ate a full meal, where was I going to take a shit? Now, I understand that the desert is like a huge kitty litter box, but damn, we were already being nasty enough by not showering and only baby wiping ourselves down. It's nothing like taking a nice shower and feeling clean, so that is why I ate one item in the MRE and lived off my Gatorade, water, and snacks from my care package. I made it my point not to shit out there in the desert unless we ran across a real camp that had a toilet. For seven months it was like that, trying to survive the elements of the desert and living in the back of the army truck (FMTV) on some foot lockers, getting up before the sun came up, and being out in the desert laying pipeline for fuel.

I must say laying the pipeline was the second hardest job I ever did for the Army. If you can imagine walking two hundred miles in the desert, laying the pipeline while it is 130 degrees and you're in full gear with your Joint Service Light Weight Intergraded chemical suit, known as the JS list, and as far as you can see you have to lay the pipeline in that direction. We had these gate valves made out of pure brass (245 alloy) that we had to connect to the pipeline every five miles. I remember a full bird Colonel from 416th Engineers Brigade who came out to the pipeline and told us how good of a job we were doing and how vital this pipeline was to the war mission. He told us if we needed anything to keep the pipeline moving smoothly to please let him know. Well, at the time I was only an E-4 Specialist and I raised my hand and said, "Sir, can we get a Bobcat with the forks attachment so that we can get the gate valves off the truck safely?"

The Colonel kind of paused for a minute and asked why we couldn't unload by hand. I told him that these valves were made out of pure brass with a 245 alloy and it cost about $20,000 to make for each gate valve in the foundry. He then asked me how I knew that. I told him when I was eighteen years old I worked in the foundry in Oakland, California. We used to make these for the Navy when the Alameda Naval Air Station was open during Desert Storm in the 1990s. Everyone looked at me like *Who in the hell is this guy?* But I didn't care what they thought of me because my interjection got us the Bobcat with the forks, and that Bobcat saved us a ton of backbreaking work.

When we laid the last pipeline for fuel, we were about one hundred miles short of Baghdad. We thought we had accomplished the mission, but we got word that we had to go all the way back to Kuwait and pick up the second trace of pipe. We were very upset because we all wondered whose idea it was to lay two traces of pipeline from Camp Virginia all the way to the Kuwait/Iraq border and lay the single trace of pipe through the Iraq desert. The one good thing about returning to Kuwait to pick up the second trace of pipe was that we were heading to a real camp with real chow hall food, showers, phones to call home—it was a taste of civilization.

We were at Camp Virginia conducting prep work to redeploy back home to Fort Sill. We ended up leaving Camp Virginia and heading to another camp to wash our vehicles and get ready to ship home to Fort Sill. This was my first time seeing a full-on twenty-four-hour Company operation on getting all of our Company's vehicles washed and having them ready to be shipped. I remember washing vehicles at six o'clock in the evening, and it was an all-night affair to stage them in a holding area, ready to be put on the ship. When morning came all vehicles were done, and we began to take them from the holding area to be loaded on the ship. By the late evening, everything was done and that was why I called it a full-on twenty-four-hour Company operation.

Later that night, we had to get all of our gear and start to process out of the country. By this time, we still didn't have a clue when we were going home or what order we were in as far as flight schedule. So they sent us from tent to tent to out-process, and it was an all-night ordeal. It was like a tent maze, and at the last tent, we saw a big, white plane on the airstrip, which we called "the bird"; it was our ride back to Fort Sill.

The Flight Home to Fort Sill, Oklahoma

During the long flight home on 7 July 2003, I slept most of the time. I believe the sleep I had during the twenty-four-hour flight was the most sleep I had had in seven months. The chartered flight made a fuel stop in Ireland, and as we got off the plane, the people in Ireland welcomed American Soldiers with open arms and told us, "Great job!" and "Enjoy your time at home." During that time, I didn't know that we, as Soldiers, were getting that much support on fighting the war on terrorism, but then again, that was our first connection to the outside world. With the warm welcome from Ireland, we were extremely hyped to reach American soil.

We flew out of Ireland heading to what I thought would be a small airport in Maine. When we arrived for another fuel stop, we got off the plane out into the gating area, and it was nice to be on American soil. We could smell the American life and oh my goodness, there were so many people in the airport greeting us. It was a great feeling but scary at the same time. Well, it wasn't scary per se, but there were so many people greeting us and hugging us all and telling us great job, but in back of my mind, I thought, *All I did was did my job as a Soldier in Iraq.* My next thought was, *Where was the warm welcome when the Soldiers came home from Vietnam?* I did like the fact the people in Maine offered their cell phone so that we could call our families to let them know that we were stateside and we were coming home.

Arriving to Lawton, Oklahoma

Our visit in Maine was an awesome experience, but I still believed all I did was my job as a Soldier. Our visit in Maine gave us Soldiers a good idea of what to expect once we arrived at Fort Sill. Once back on the plane, I tried my best to get some sleep on this last trip home to Fort Sill, but I couldn't sleep because I was so excited about arriving home and seeing my family again. We finally arrived to some type of hole-in-the-wall airport in Lawton, Oklahoma. The airport was so small that I never knew it existed until we landed there. As we exited the plane and breathed in the Oklahoma air, we all wondered, *Where in the hell is our family?* At first, we all thought that the dates got screwed up about our arrival. There wasn't one person at the airport to greet us from Fort Sill, other than the bus to take us to Fort Sill for "the dog and pony show ceremony" (the welcome home ceremony.

The airport was about seven miles or so outside the city of Lawton, so the bus ride seemed pretty long. But even though we were confused about where our families were, it was nice to be back in Lawton. As we approached the city limits, the town looked pretty dead. I mean it was a good day to sit back and watch the grass grow. It wasn't until we drove onto Fort Sill Boulevard and crossed Cache Boulevard that we started to see civilization. I remember an old Vietnam Vet ran in front of the bus and made the bus driver come to complete stop. The Vietnam Vet asked permission to ride with us on the bus. He stated that he was proud of us Soldiers who went to Iraq to kick ass and take names and accomplished the mission. During that time, we started to see the people of Lawton holding up banner signs saying: "Welcome home!" "Great job," and "We miss you." By this time, we started to feel the welcome home feeling but still wanted to see our families. After entering Fort Sill, we finally arrived to where the dog and pony show was supposed to happen. Most of us Soldiers don't like these welcome home ceremonies, only because all we want to do is grab our bags, find our loved ones, and go home. Besides, our welcome home celebration actually started in the confined space of our bedroom.

After the ceremony was over, we were released to search for our loved ones. It took me a few minutes because I forgot what my family looked like. I spent seven months looking at Soldiers in Desert uniform, and it almost felt like searching for a person I had never seen before. I did find my loved ones, or should I say they found me—my baby girl, age two, gave me the biggest hugs ever, and seeing her pretty smile made the worst day in hell look so good. My wife was so happy to see that her Soldier boy made it home in one piece. She noticed that I lost a ton of weight, and I told her that the 130-degree weather was no joke and laying two hundred miles of pipeline for fuel was a pretty tough job. During this moment, I felt extremely proud of myself that I did my job well during a wartime situation. My wife could hold her head up high because she knew that her Soldier boy had done his job well for our country.

As we got into our vehicles heading home, I decided I wanted to make my homecoming visit to my favorite fast food restaurant, McDonald's. You have to understand, there wasn't any sight of McDonald's while laying pipeline for fuel in the desert. We finally went home after having McDonald's with good food in my system. During our seventy-two-hour downtime, you would think I would be home resting and enjoying my family. Well, I didn't stay home; I knew a carpet layer who was shorthanded on a job so I took the time to help him out and complete the job. He couldn't believe that I had just gotten home the day prior and wanted to lay carpet. I had to do something because it was hard to work twelve to fifteen hours a day for seven months and come home without a job to do.

Getting Back into Garrison

Adjusting to Garrison life at Fort Sill was kind of tough. We had some Soldiers in our unit hiding in the rear with the gear for seven months. For some reason or another, they found some bullshit reason on not to deploy with us. *I thought, What is your sole purpose in the Army? I hope it wasn't to go to college.* Being back in Garrison was a tough adjustment after being in Iraq for seven months, but I still felt proud to be in my uniform wearing my first combat patch and that I completed the mission that the Army called me to do. I decided that I should go for my Sergeant stripes, so since I had seven months of combat experience, I started studying for the E-5 promotion board. I spent about thirty days studying. When the day arrived for the promotion board, I was nervous just like any other E-4 would be. I answered all the tough questions and somehow the answers I thought I didn't know came out smoothly. I believe I made it through all the questions due to my past experience of war.

Two months went by and my First Sergeant came to me and said, "Hey, Sergeant Duckworth, what do you know about drinking Mai Tai on the beach?"

Now at 0530, just before PT, I had no clue what he was getting at, thinking he mistook me as a Sergeant when I was still an E-4 Specialist. Come to find out I was getting promoted to E-5 Sergeant on 01 Feb 2004, and I had orders to go to Hawaii to be assigned to 84th Engineers at Schofield Barracks in Hawaii. Most of my fellow buddies thought I was one of the luckiest Soldier in the United States Army. They all asked, "How in the hell did you pull that off?"

I told them I didn't and that in fact I didn't want to be stationed in Hawaii. I knew what was ahead of me because I knew the location of each Engineer Battalion in the Army. Three of the Battalions were in Iraq and two in Afghanistan. For some reason, the 84th Engineer

Battalion was the last Battalion to leave for Iraq. Yet this Engineer Battalion was the hard-charging, fast-paced, never-daunted, get'er done-type of Battalion. Since I was newly E-5, I was going to that Battalion. I was home eight months from my first tour to Iraq and knew my report date was March 2004.

When I arrived with my family in Hawaii, on 20 March 2004, the Battalion was already in Iraq conducting construction missions. I had two months to get my family settled into housing and have our vehicles on the island. I really wasn't too thrilled to be on the island other than being at the beach, but hell that shit gets old two weeks later.

Two months later, I flew back to Iraq to meet up with the Battalion. When I arrived to Camp Anaconda, I wished the Army would have just let me stay in Iraq the first time and wait for the Battalion to arrive because as soon as my boots touched the Iraqi sand, it felt as if I'd never left. From that day forward, I did three more tours with the 84th Engineer Battalion and each tour was back to back.

In May 2004, at Camp Anaconda (a.k.a. Balad), I was with Bravo Company 84th Engineer. Mortar rounds came in on a daily basis. Most mortar rounds were hitting chow halls at dinner time, but a mortar round came in very close to our construction work site. First and Second Platoons were sent out to construct a concrete landing pad for all the Chinooks at the airfield. At the end of one of our massive concrete pours, the Platoon Sergeant asked the Non-Commissioned Officers (NCOs) to stay back to set up the battle boards for the next job site. Well, we did and we ran string lines to set up for form work. We ran out of string lines and one of my fellow NCOs said that she would go look in the tool trailer to see if we had one. As she was walking toward the trailer, a mortar round was coming, and for the first time I saw it. I tried to yell out the Sergeant's name, but the words couldn't come out of my mouth at all. The mortar round went over our job site and landed about seventy-five meters from us. She turned and looked at me, saw that I was in shock and couldn't get any words out, and we all said, "Fuck this shit, we are out of here!"

We went back to our Platoon Sergeant and gave a report of what happened. A week went by and a F16 fighter jet flying low sounded like a mortar round coming in. Of course, I couldn't see the F16 flying low, but the sound was really loud. I got scared and ran away from the project site. A fellow NCO saw me running and asked me where I was going. I said that I heard that loud noise and thought it was a mortar round coming in. She said no, it was an F16 landing. By then, she kind of laughed at me, and I knew that I could never show any weakness, especially since I was a fellow NCO.

In July or August 2004, at Camp Anaconda, the main Post Exchange (PX) got hit by a mortar round twice during lunchtime. I was walking toward the PX prior to the mortar rounds hitting the PX. I had been wanting to go there for the last two days, but one of my fellow NCOs stopped me. He said, "Hey, Sergeant Duckworth, I got those pictures you have been asking for and I've e-mailed them to you."

I told him thank you very much. I was closer to the Internet café than I was the PX, so I went to the Internet café. As soon as I walked in, a mortar round hit so hard that it shook the concrete building I was in, but it had actually hit the PX a half a block away. Then a second one hit and after that we all left and headed to our units for accountability. Still to this day, I think that my fellow NCO was looking out for me by stopping me from heading to the PX; I would not be here today if it wasn't for him.

In July or August 2004, Camp Anaconda ALFA Company 84th Engineers lost five vehicles and one generator in one week by mortar rounds having a lock on the ALFA company area. I asked the Company's First Sergeant when he was going to have the Company relocated because his area was a hot zone. He stated that he was trying but there wasn't any support to get them a new place, and they never did. In 2006, Bravo Company 84th Engineers took that same building, and I told them that this place was a hot zone for mortar rounds due to what happened to ALFA Company in 2004. They didn't listen to me, but as the deployment went on, it finally happened.

One morning, a few Soldiers and I were trying to figure out what we should do for PT. I told them we should head to the gym because I knew we would feel safe over there, but some of my Soldiers wanted to go on a run. I told them we were heading to the gym, so we started walking to the gym, and when we got there about four minutes later a mortar round hit very close. We didn't know where it hit. After everything was over, we headed back to the Company and came to find out the mortar round hit on the side of our building and knocked out a five thousand-gallon water tank. When the mortar round hit the ground, river rocks ended up being embedded into trees near our Company area. This was the same area we were standing in prior to us deciding what we were doing for PT.

January 2006, Camp LSA Anaconda

I was tasked out to do body searches on Iraqi people in order for them to come into our camp to do work throughout the day; it was a thirty-day detail. The daily activities consisted of reporting at 0500, getting a morning briefing at 0600, and at 0700 get transported to the entry gate where we had to do our morning body searches. We searched between 100 and 250 Iraqis, looking in their lunch bags for contraband. Every day I did the body search, it made me feel extremely bad. I didn't like touching another male, knowing that they had not bathed in months, and the body odor they had was awful. If you had a big breakfast, it would be coming up before the body search was over, and this was in the middle of January. It was really cold outside so I didn't understand how they could have such bad body odor, knowing that there was a river that ran through their villages. If it were mid-July, then I could see how the bad body odor could accrue. Now come to think of it, I can see how I ended up testing positive for tuberculosis after my third tour, and I had to do that task twice throughout my deployment. Anyhow, after we were all done with the body searches, they got transported to this holding area to get broken down into groups. There were two Soldiers to every sixteen Iraqis, and we would get the detailed information on where they would be working at on post. Most of the jobs were picking up trash and stuff like that. Some of the Iraqi people were pretty cool and some were just average working people, just trying to make a buck. The funny thing was that most of them had eight to twelve wives. There was one crazy Iraqi guy who somehow had the balls to come up to me and tell me that he liked sheep. I told him that I had not eaten sheep before, and I hadn't had lamb chops for dinner. Later he told me that he liked sheep very much, and I told him again that was cool. I told him that my daughter loved animals and she wanted to be an animal doctor so she could take care of the animals when they were sick. He looked at me and smiled and continued to work. Later, his friend came up to me and told me that his friend liked sheep. When I indicated that I understood this fact, he said, "No, you don't understand. He has five wives but he likes having sex with sheep."

I felt sick and pissed off that I had an Iraqi guy in my work group that liked to have sex with sheep. I was more pissed off because I carried on the conversation, not knowing where it was going. I told his friend to stop playing and get back to work, but he told me that he was telling the truth. He asked his friend in front of me if he liked having sex with sheep and he nodded his head yes, with a big smile. Everyone was laughing and I had to shake my head in disbelief and look at this guy, knowing that he liked to have sex with sheep. I didn't understand why I had to know this, but he worked in my work group three different times throughout the thirty days.

A few days later, I had another Iraqi guy that I really had to watch. I had seen him around at different work groups and each time he was always happy, making jokes with his friends, and making jokes around the Soldiers. But when he came to my work group, I noticed that when we did our body search that he had a different attitude. He did not speak to anyone and worked alone, not with the group. I remember another Soldier told him to do something and he wouldn't respond. Well, later toward the end of the day, I pulled him aside, along with the translator, and asked the translator what was going on; I wanted to know what was wrong and maybe I could help him. He told the translator that my people had shot his father, and when the translator told me that, I said no, my people didn't shoot his dad. At the time, I was thinking about my fellow Soldiers in my Platoon, but he mentioned that it was the United States Army Soldiers in the same uniform as me who shot his father, and he was in the hospital in this camp.

I told him that I didn't think that his dad would be in the hospital in this camp because just last week I was in the same hospital. In the trauma center, I saw nothing but American contractors who were truck drivers who were attacked in an ambush. Some of the truck drivers had multiple gunshots; one had been shot in the head but was somehow still alive. I thought, *What the hell are we doing?* And what I meant about that was, *What the fuck were our Soldiers doing to allow this to happen to our contractors?* I felt really bad and I wished I could help or do something; all I knew was that it was a mess with blood everywhere. For the first time, I felt ashamed to wear the United States Army uniform because it felt like we weren't doing enough to protect American contractors and these contractors brought in all of the supplies to various camps to Soldiers and Airmen. My thought was, *This is the best we can do to protect them?!* After looking at what I saw in the trauma center, it seemed like we weren't doing shit for convoy security. Anyhow, I did agree to take the translator and this young man to the hospital and look for his dad. When we went to the same trauma center where I was the week before, the scenery had changed drastically. This time I saw nothing but Iraqi personnel who were shot. Some had two shots in the stomach, some were shot in the shoulder, and some were just all around shot up.

There were two who were shot in the head; one was a little girl who was age seven, but she was alive. I wondered, *How did she get caught in the crosshairs of someone's scope?* The other person who was shot in the head was the worker's dad.

Now, you have to stop and think that yes, I was happy to see that some Iraqis were in the trauma center with gunshot wounds due to my fellow Soldiers who were kicking some ass at the moment. But when you have a young man right beside you, regardless what race he is or what part of the world he is from, feelings change when you see the young boy holding his father with a gunshot wound to the head. It really makes you think, *Man, that could have been my dad*, and I hoped that someone would help me get my dad out the hospital if the situation happened to me.

This young man wanted to get his dad out of the hospital, even though he wasn't in good condition to leave. But he was still asking for my help to get him out. I informed him that the doctors agreed that his dad should not be released from the hospital to go home. The doctor also informed him that his dad would be transported to the Iraqi hospital in Bagdad, so he could continue to get more treatment and later he would be sent home. The young man was happy and showed a little sign of relief. He thanked me for allowing him to see his dad. I saw the young man a few more times, but his father was still in the hospital in Bagdad; I hoped they were all doing okay. I did try my best to help out any way I could because I knew that the people in Iraq always thought of us United States Army Soldiers as nothing but a bunch of killers who destroyed anything that was in our way in order for us to get to our destination and complete our mission. However, we cared for people regardless of the situation.

In December 2006, the first Platoon from Bravo Company 84th Engineers was close to heading home after spending a year at Camp LSA Anaconda. Our minds were set on going home, and we were kind of getting too relaxed for the environment we were in. We were twenty days out from leaving Camp Anaconda, but some last construction order had come in for us to go down to Baghdad to Camp Victory to build one last building. I asked during the briefing, "Why do we have to go when engineers are already down there?"

I was told there was a vertical construction unit down there, but they built this one building and it took them forty-five days to complete the job. That unit was Charlie Company 411 Engineers. I told my chain of command that I didn't like that unit; they were shitty Engineers. I didn't like them when they were at Fort Wainwright, Alaska, back in 1998, and I didn't like them today. We went down there and built the same size building and it took us twelve days to complete the same building they were building.

On the way down to Baghdad in a convoy, the vehicle behind us had trouble with the brake system; it kept locking up on him. We had to come to a complete halt to see if we could fix the problem. It was late at night, like 0100 or 0200 in the morning, pitch black with a few houses in the area. When the convoy was stopped to fix the problem, an unknown vehicle approached us from the front. I radioed to the Convoy Commander to let them know that a vehicle was approaching us that wasn't allowed anywhere in or around our convoy. When the vehicle passed, I radioed again, requesting permission to shoot the unknown vehicle. The permission was granted, and I told my gunner to shoot that motherfucker; my gunner had a 249 Squad automatic weapon and shot off maybe twenty to thirty rounds. The Convoy Commander reported back to hold fire and allow the vehicle to go through. I didn't understand why but we had to follow orders and allow the unknown vehicle to pass through. Vehicles like the one we encountered are subject to have Improvised Explosive Devices (IEDs) loaded in their vehicle waiting to set off to dismantle a convoy. By then, I radioed back asking request to help out on the broken down truck that we had, and my Squad Leader got on the radio and informed me to drop my trailer and go across the median to watch for IED and go and hook up the broken down truck so we could move out. I said, "Roger that," and I told my driver what we had to do. She got scared and said that she couldn't do it. I told her to jump out of the driver seat and I would drive so that we could get this shit done. I dropped my trailer but as I was getting out I kept leaving the door open, leaving my fellow NCOs and my gunner exposed to a Rocket-Propelled Grenade, (RPG) that could possibly kill my Soldiers and destroy the cab of our truck. My fellow NCOs kept yelling at me saying that it defeated the purpose of having armored doors if I was going to leave the door open every time I got out. I kind of felt bad because a simple mistake like that could get someone killed and it would be my fault. But at the same time, if my other fellow NCO would have done his preventive maintenance checks and servicing (PMCS), he would have noticed something wrong with the brakes. I didn't have time to be upset or mad; I just had to complete the mission so we all could move out. When I got the truck in position and met up with the driver, the first thing he told me was that his truck had been acting funny for the past two days. All I could do was look at him as if he was the douche bag of the century and get his truck hooked up so we could move out. I got his truck hooked up to my truck and my trailer to his truck. I radioed back to our Squad Leader to let her know that we were ready to roll, and we continued the convoy mission.

We were doing fine and were up to sixty miles per hour, but I noticed that the temperature on the transmission was getting kind of high, so we had to let the convoy know that we couldn't maintain that speed due to the weight that I was carrying. We went from sixty miles per hour to twenty-five, all the way to Baghdad. We made it safely, but I tell you this: I never spoke to that fellow NCO who couldn't do a proper PMCS on his truck, who had every one's lives on the line because he didn't do his job. And with my female NCO, I told her that I was sorry I kept leaving the armored door wide open. I always told her that even after our fourth tour to Iraq, it seemed like I was almost getting to the point to where I didn't trust people do to their jobs. People don't understand how important it is to do their job right and pay attention to details because if you don't, people can die.

Mosul, Iraq, 2008

Prior to Mosul 2008, a fellow NCO who was with 523rd 84th Engineers in Schofield Barracks. This NCO. would go out of his way to say, "Hello, Sergeant Duckworth, how are you doing?" Or maybe we would be in a situation where he was in a crowd of people in the Company area and would go out of his way and speak to me. Still to this day, I don't understand why he spoke to me. We weren't buddies nor had we ever served together at a different duty station.

When we arrived to Mosul on 01 December 2008, I knew it was going to be a long fourth tour for me. The place looked dull and gloomy, and you could taste and smell of war in the air, almost like smelling death. Since we had arrived to Mosul to replace the other unit, we had to do this thing called the "left seat, right seat" ride. In other words, the old unit had to show us how things were going outside the wire, and the new unit had to sit in the right seat and learn how things went outside the wire. This particular NCO from the 523rd was in one of the vehicles and a car bomb got in between the convoy at a circle intersection, known as Baghdad Circle. The car bomb exploded and killed everyone in the Mine Resistant Ambush Protection Vehicle, known as the MRAP along with the NCO who always went out of his way to speak to me (RIP, Sergeant). When the car bomb exploded and brought the MRAP to its knees, the insurgents finally knew how many explosives to use to bring something like the MRAP down. This vehicle costs the US tax payers over one million dollars to make, along with updated protective vehicle armor for the vehicle.

When I found out that he had died in that explosion, I knew it was going to be a long deployment. I had to make sure I did my job to the fullest to where I didn't get anyone killed, and I had to watch for my Platoon Sergeant. He was a Sergeant First Class (SFC E-7) and it was his first time to Iraq, along with our Platoon Leader (First Lieutenant). I had mixed emotions about my Platoon Sergeant. How could a person like me do four tours to Iraq and here was this SFC just now coming to Iraq for the first time? How was I supposed to take guidance from him? Things worked out pretty well; I made sure that the Platoon Sergeant and the Platoon Leader didn't have to worry about me not completing my mission because I made sure I did my job. My biggest worry was watching the Platoon Sergeant and the Platoon Leader do their jobs right. After all, it was their first time to Iraq, and I hoped that they listened to those of us who had been there three or four times. Things worked out pretty well in the First Platoon 643rd. At that time, the Soldiers in the 643rd First Platoon were the only people I trusted, and they all trusted me.

Mosul, Iraq, 25 December 2008

For the entire day starting on 25 December 2008, I thought the war had started all over again like in January 2003 during my first tour. Mortar rounds just kept coming in all over Camp Marez. All I could think of was that it was going to be a long deployment and it was my fourth tour. There was a dictum that was told to us: when you were on your third tour you were lucky to be alive, and when you were on your fourth tour it was as if your time was going to be up any minute. In other words, your life was on borrowed time, and that was how I felt the whole duration of my fourth deployment: "on borrowed time." Mortar rounds kept coming all day and night Christmas Day. It was so bad that going to the chow hall was the last thing on my mind. The last time I was in a situation like this was in Camp Anaconda during my second and third tour, and mortar rounds were hitting the chow halls. There were times when I didn't eat dinner chow for six weeks, and I only lived off of care packages that my mother in-law sent. I was scared on that day but at the same time it made me angry because the mortar rounds were coming in and we couldn't do anything about it. I just wanted to go outside the wire and just shoot anything that moved and ask questions later. After all, I did have 210 rounds for my M16. December 25 was the longest day of my life, just like when the war started back in March 2003. That had been the longest thirty-six hours of my life with no sleep, and even sleep would be the last thing on my mind; my number one priority was staying alive.

Somewhere Outside of
Mosul, Covert Denial Mission

On this mission, I can't remember how many covert denial missions we'd done, but it was during January and February 2009. A covert denial mission is a mission where you go out and stop the insurgents from loading IEDs into the covert that could blow up the roads that we used each and every day. So Forward Support Command (FSC) from that 84th Engineer Battalion would make the cages out of angle iron and no. 4 rebar, and those of us from 1st Platoon from 643rd would anchor bolt them to the concrete walls and weld the nuts to the anchor bolts, which would stop the covert denial access. On this one mission, the Iraqi translator was on the convoy with us, and on this particular night we were working on one side of the covert. My Palletized Load System (M1075 PLS) driver was using the Bobcat to get the loose dirt out away from the concrete wall so our cages could fit tightly against the wall. That job was done pretty quickly so our Warrant Officer told us to go across the road to remove the loose dirt. It was really dark and the only light I had was the flashlight and whatever light we had on the Bobcat. When we approached the other side, I saw some dogs and I thought they were pretty brave to just be laying there. As I got down in the covert, I saw more dogs. Come to find out this covert was rigged up with IEDs and it was in the body parts of dogs. There were about fifteen to twenty dogs; some were missing heads and some had their whole insides just turned inside out. I figured that these dogs were at the wrong place at the wrong time but that these IEDs were for us. By that time, I came out of the covert and told my Soldier to get back to the PLS. I didn't tell him what I saw; I just told him to get back to the PLS.

As we got across the road by our PLS, my mind was still on the dogs that were blown up with missing heads, and my Soldier and I saw the translator by our PLS. My Soldier and I looked at each other, wondering what the hell was this translator doing by our truck? At this point, I was glad I didn't have my weapon on me; my weapon was in the cab of the PLS, but the translator was kneeling down by the back tire. I wondered if he was planting an IED by my truck. And again my mind was still on those damn dogs that had been blown up, and I didn't know if there were any more IEDs on that side of the covert. I grabbed the translator, turned him around, slammed him against my truck, and asked him, "What the fuck are you doing by my truck!"

He got scared and said, "Oh God, I'm sorry. I didn't mean to do it."

I asked, "What the fuck did you do?" And as I was asking him that question, I was looking around the tires of my truck to see if he planted an IED. He said he was sorry, he had to go pee, and he didn't mean to piss on my truck; he wasn't trying to disrespect the United States Army vehicle by using it as a restroom. What really bothered me was that we as Soldiers were trained to understand the culture and the language of the Iraqi people, but no one ever told us how they peed outside in the desert. If American men had to pee, they stood up and went behind a tree or a truck. This Iraqi translator was about to get shot because I thought he was planting an IED on my truck, but luckily my weapon was in the cab of my truck. I told the translator that I was sorry for grabbing him the way I did. As you can see, I didn't take any mess from anyone, and I wasn't taking any chances. Like I said, on your fourth tour to Iraq, your life is on borrowed time and borrowed time is so limited, it seemed.

Mosul, Iraq, 2009

My Soldier and I were the operators for the PLS. When our Platoon came back for another camp farther up north, he and I were called out to go on another mission with 84th Engineers HSC. At that time, we had been gone from Camp Marez for forty-five days, and we weren't in camp six hours before we had to go out with HSC. Well, my Soldier had found me at the chow hall at dinner time and informed me that he and I had to go out on a mission. I asked him what mission he was talking about. He informed me that we had to fill a pothole where the Lieutenant Colonel and his Soldier had died from an IED blast earlier that day. During that time, I wasn't mad or pissed off. I said, "Let's do this."

So I went to the Platoon office to get the briefing and when I went in, the whole office was quiet. I didn't know why but I guessed they thought I was going to be mad and upset, talking about why I had to go and that it was bullshit, but I didn't say those things. The Soldier and I met up with HSC with the PLS and got ahold of the concrete module and started loading up the water tanks, sand, rocks, and other stuff. We rolled out with 84th HSC at 2300hrs and rolled into downtown Mosul. If anyone tells you about Mosul, they will say that place is a hellhole, but to me "a hellhole" is an understatement. When we arrived to the pothole, it was so big that you could take a Chevy Tahoe and bury it and you wouldn't miss it. I got out of the truck and tried to help the guys pour the concrete so we could get out of there, but they told me they got it and they wanted me to man the radio in my PLS.

We were there for quite some time and I decided to get out of my PLS to stretch my legs, when all of a sudden, an IED went off about a hundred meters from me and I jumped back in to the PLS and radioed in to the Convoy Commander that an IED went off and we needed to roll out before the next one went off. The response that I got back was that we were to stand our ground and stay until the concrete dried. Now you have to understand what situation I was in. I was thirty-nine years old at the time on my fourth tour to Iraq, and I had to listen to some damn Lieutenant who was on his first tour to Iraq. Everyone in the Construction Engineering field in the United States Army in Iraq knows that when you order concrete in Iraq, you make sure that this one additive is added in to the concrete to let the concrete harden up fast, and that didn't happen. When my Platoon (First Platoon in 643rd 84th Engineer Battalion) went on a pothole mission, my Platoon Sergeant and my Platoon Leader made sure we added the Quick Crete into the concrete so it could harden up fast. When we were done pouring and smoothing the concrete out, after putting our company logo on it, we would have the Iraqi interpreter inform the Iraqi police to ask for someone to watch the concrete dry while we moved on out to the next hole or the next mission. But that didn't happen when I was with 84th HSC.

By that time I had to listen to this Lieutenant who didn't know shit, and that's when I called it quits after fourteen years of service and four tours to Iraq. It seemed like leaders and managers didn't know what their jobs were or just didn't care. When we got back to Camp Marez, I went to find that LT so I could have a few words with him. My few words would have consisted of putting my hands on an Officer. Since I couldn't find him, I waited until my Platoon Sergeant and Platoon Leader let them know what had happened on that mission. When I saw them and told them we had to stay out there and wait for the concrete to dry, my Platoon Leader got so upset that she left the office and went and told the Company Commander. I don't know what happened after that, but somehow I later received a combat action badge. That was okay but the main problem I had was with the LT. I had to trust his decision and have faith that he knew his job, but I guess he didn't and today this is the reason why I don't trust leaders, managers, or other authorities. But if I allowed a Soldier to go on a mission without his proper gear and if he got hurt or killed, I would be the one going to jail for life. As an

NCO, I'm supposed to do my job as a professional Non-Commission Officer, and Officers (Lieutenants and above) who don't get their feet held to the fire just move on.

Another Mosul Moment

This event occurred sometime in the summertime when I was out in Diamond Back, just right across from Camp Marez. Camp Marez and Camp Diamond Back were just like Schofield Barracks and Wheeler Airfield. We built seven sea huts on Diamond Back, and I was installing the ductless units of the one-ton air conditioning unit in one of the rooms inside the sea hut, without any warning, there was a loud blast. A blast so bad that the wall inside the sea hut came in and went back out. At the same time, I was on the ladder trying to mount the head unit onto the wall, but the blast was so huge that the impact knocked me off the ladder. I tried to save the head unit from falling to the ground, which I did, so the head unit wasn't damaged.

Later that day when we were done with work, we went back to Camp Marez and I went into the operations area and told the operation NCO that the blast was huge. He asked me if I wanted to see what happened and I said yes. He also asked me if I had a security clearance and I said yes (I had just gotten it in March), so he pulled it up on the big screen. What I saw was a convoy that was approaching Diamond Back and an unknown twenty-ton dump truck was approaching them when the gunner in the convoy shot at the driver in the twenty-ton truck. The driver in the truck died but the truck still kept rolling, and it veered off the road and hit the side of the building. The twenty-ton truck exploded and killed everyone in the convoy. Camp Marez and Diamond Back shook like the bad earthquake back in 1989 in California, and come to find out there were ten thousand pounds' worth of explosives in that twenty-ton truck.

Stop Sign Mission

I can't remember where in Iraq, but it was south of Mosul by a tall bridge. The main focus was a temporary bridge down below the tall bridge running across the Tigris River. A mission came down to 1st Platoon to where we had to put a posted sign for a 25 mph speed limit on a temporary bridge that was installed by a bridge unit two years prior. Now, I am all for going outside the wire to do a mission, but to go on a mission for some darn speed signs by a bridge that had been sitting for two years, that's asking for a big death wish. I mean why now? Why was it *that* day we had to put up that posted sign? Well, I never asked or called it out as bullshit, but I knew it had to be done. When we arrived there, we did our normal security standpoint, blocking roads using our MRAP vehicles with the .50 caliber high-powered weapon along with other gunners locked and loaded, also with the RG33 blocking the other side of the road. We downloaded the PLS flatbed trailer and got the Bobcat ready and attached the earth auger to the Bobcat and started drilling holes every hundred meters to put the signs in. In operating the Bobcat, I was the best man for the job. I didn't have time to bullshit, and there was a lot of opportunity for anything to go wrong with this mission, like an RPG hitting the Bobcat with me in it and having me, or my body parts, wash down the river.

I was going across the engineer bridge that had been sitting there for two years, and the Bobcat could only go five or eight miles per hour, full throttle. All I could think of was, *Shit, I hope no RPG comes shooting at me.* Later I was thinking about what plan of action I should take if that occurred. I can't remember how many signs we had to put in, but it was a lot. When we put the last one in, I was by the Platoon Sergeant and I told him that was the last one. He said good and I told him that I was going to take the Bobcat back to the

PLS, load it up, and turn the PLS around, ready to roll out. Something came in through the radio that said there was some trouble at the security point that we had set up. Come to find out that there were 250 Iraqi Soldiers waiting to get to Baghdad, and if they didn't get to Baghdad in time, they wouldn't get paid until next month. Well, the NCOs and the translator tried to explain what we were doing, and a few Iraqi Soldiers tried to act up like they wanted to do something. The gunner in the MRAP had his .50 caliber pointed toward the crowd, and they ran and hid in their cars. While all this was going on, I tried to get the Bobcat loaded up really fast and have the PLS turn around and head into the right direction so we could head out.

My biggest fear with this mission was that it was 250 Iraqi Soldiers and only thirty personnel from the First Platoon, and we almost started a mini war with the Iraqi Soldiers over a speed sign. It always made me wonder how these Officers could take on stupid missions like this and put our Soldiers' lives on the line for some damn signs. It seemed like Officers would do what it took to make their career look good, but they forgot that it was the Soldiers who made their careers look good—that's why the NCOs are the backbone of the Army. When we got back to Camp Marez, put down our gear, and got accountability on all sensitive items, I spoke to my Platoon Leader. I told her to please not accept a stupid mission like that again. I told her that I didn't have the time or the patience to put up with stupid missions like that, especially when I was on my fourth tour in Iraq. I also mentioned to her that I would go out and do the entire road repair missions that came down to us, but do not accept anything that involved the posted sign missions. She looked at me and said, "Sergeant Duckworth, that would be the last stupid mission from the chain of command." In my mind, I hoped it was worth it and that we made someone's career look good.

The Invisible Wound from War

On December 1, 2009, I was happy to be home and thought that the people in my condo area would welcome me. My next-door neighbor welcomed me back. I told him what I did In Iraq, and he said he wanted to add a bedroom in his condo. I told him I could do the work, and I educated him on what needed to happen. He told me that he would let me know when he was ready. I told him that the only problem was that we needed to match the color of the shingles on the roof, but I would find out what that was.

Later that day, I saw another neighbor. I was looking at her roof and telling her how I just got home from Iraq, conducting construction missions and road repairs. She said, "Welcome back," with an unenthusiastic attitude. I told her that my next-door neighbor wanted me to do an add-on to his condo in the backyard. She asked me if I was a contractor. I looked at her as if she were stupid because I had just told her I'd returned home from Iraq conducting various construction missions and road repairs. I told her no I wasn't a contractor, and she went on saying that I couldn't do an add-on if I wasn't a licensed contractor. By then, I kind of lost my cool and told her, "Look ma'am, you mean to tell me that I'm good enough to put my life on the line to protect this country and fight to protect your freedom and your way of life?" I also mentioned to her that I had built a total of eighty thousand square feet of living space and office space for our fellow Soldiers and coalition forces and have conducted over five thousand miles of road repairs due to IED blasts. Not to mention, I still did my job while being fired upon—mortar rounds dropping around us. I told her when all that shit was going on, no one tapped me on the shoulder and said, "Excuse me, Sergeant Duckworth, but are you a licensed contractor to build all these buildings in Iraq?" I told that bitch to go to hell and "enjoy your freedom."

I was so mad that my left shoulder went numb and my chest was on fire. From that day on, that was my first clue to let me know that the American people didn't care what I did in Iraq. They did not even give me credit for the job experience that I had in the military. There are tons of licensed contractors on this island, but not one could do what I did or go through what I went through in Iraq.

For starters, they would have to withstand the 130-degree weather and a lot of them wouldn't last a day. I had been there and did that four different times, but she had the nerve to ask me if I was a licensed contractor to build one bedroom! It was a damn shame that I could build all that shit in Iraq, but I needed to be licensed to do an add-on to someone's house. I can tell you this: the American people who want to undermine the skills I had in the military can go and fuck themselves. Building a total of eighty thousand square feet of living space in one year's time in combat conditions is way more what an average contractor would do in his hometown. I read on the Internet that sometime in 2009, a famous basketball player had his house built in Florida, and it was a total of thirty-eight thousand square feet. That should tell you that my Platoon had put in double or triple the work of those contractors who built the house for that ball player. It seems like the Army should have come up with some type of program where we could be licensed or certified. I mean, I installed two hundred of the split units heating and air conditioning for the buildings that we had built with no license, but I had to do it knowing that the construction company from the Houston area that were in Iraq had licensed A/C guys to install the units for us. Somehow they didn't do it, knowing they were making somewhere between ten and fifteen grand a month working on A/C. My Engineer Unit handed out Freon like it was candy. At the same time back in the States, in order to handle Freon you had to be licensed. People like me had orders to put our lives on the line doing construction missions and anything else that followed, like installing air conditioning. But I came home from Iraq with all these skills and no license, and no one would give me a job regardless of my skills and experience while serving our country. Still to this day I don't have a job, but I do have a shitload of construction tools and a truck with nowhere to go. I still say, "What the fuck did I go to Iraq for?"

I know why I went to Iraq. I had to follow orders, but after being home, I have felt like a third-class citizen, which triggers me to think that the American citizens are the enemies. I have just gotten to the point where I don't know what the American people want these days.

On December 31, 2009, I was at Long's Drug Store in Kapolei, Hawaii. I was already on edge because everyone wanted to start firing off their fireworks, and some of the fireworks were really loud explosions like the IEDs that went off, and they made me feel as if I never left Iraq.

There was a lady in front of me at the cash register with a shopping cart full of fireworks. I asked the lady where she lived, and she told me Nanakuli. I told her that she didn't realize how much trauma she brought to Soldiers who lived in her neighborhood. She asked what I meant by that, and I told her there were Soldiers who were coming home from Iraq and the last thing they wanted to hear were some fireworks going off as if they were still in Iraq. As I was telling her about it, I felt so much anger and rage in me because I felt like people didn't have any respect for us Soldiers coming from Iraq. All we asked for was a little peace and quiet. The lady looked at me and saw that I was not playing about what I said. By then, she had nothing to say about the amount of fireworks she had bought. She paid for the fireworks and walked away.

Later that day, I was in Kapolei at a Shell gas station getting some gas. While I was pumping gas, I noticed that the hose was dry and rotted, and the rubber portion was peeling off. At the same time, a person ahead of me was pumping gas as well, but she was talking on her cell while pumping gas. I finished pumping my gas, and I walked up to the lady and explained to her that I had just gotten home from completing four tours in Iraq. I explained to her that there was a sign in front of her that said no cell phone use while pumping gas. She looked at me as if I was crazy, but I told her that I would not get blown up at a gas station just because she wanted to talk on the phone. I told her she didn't understand how it felt to have ten thousand pounds of explosives go off when you're less than a quarter of a mile away. At that time, I was in a rage and ready to fight her. My chest was burning as if it was on fire, and I was having trouble breathing. At the last moment, I walked in and told the person at the cash register about the fuel hose dry-rotting and that they needed to shut the pump down and get it fixed. However, I talked to them as if they were Soldiers; I was the NCO telling them that they needed to do a better job, not just to be here to collect a paycheck.

Seconds later, a customer came in to pay for the gas, and they reported that the hose they were using was leaking fuel and his pants were wet from the fuel. Now, I may have been wrong for talking to them the way I did, but I had seen an unsafe act at the gas station, and I was in fear that my life was on the line as well as others. I was frustrated that the workers did substandard work when I was in Iraq as a Soldier. I put in all of my effort to fight the war on terrorism and protect their freedom and their way of life. I hated to see an average worker having a job in customer service and conducting poor quality work.

Around two the afternoon, my daughter and I were at home in Makakilo. By that time, the loud exploding sounds of the fireworks were getting worse. They were going off every twenty minutes, and it sounded like there were right outside of my door because the front door was open. I went to see where it came from, and my next-door neighbor came out; it was scaring him as well. I told my neighbor that if I caught someone firing off those loud fireworks, I was going to beat their ass. I told him that I was sorry I felt that way, but at home, those sounds sounded like an explosion. The next two went off so loudly that it set off two car alarms that were about one hundred meters from my front door, and it scared the shit out of me. I was in my La-Z-Boy chair watching a show, and my heart started to race. By then, I grabbed my work gloves and walked outside looking to seeing who had set another one off. I walked around and headed toward a blue house and asked the owner who was setting those fireworks off. He told me that it was coming from up the street. So I walked back to my house, still fired up and ready to fight. I told my daughter to come with me because we were going for a little ride. We got in the car, with me wearing my work gloves, and we rode up and down the neighborhood looking for the people who were firing off the fireworks. I didn't find anyone, and I was kind of glad because they would be in the hospital and I would be in jail.

Later that night, my wife asked me if I wanted to go to one of our friends' houses to set off fireworks. I told her no because of the issues I was going through that day. She and my daughter went and I stayed home by myself; I locked myself in the bedroom. I had on earplugs, but it didn't help. It was loud and crazy and it made me very angry because I couldn't go out and beat anyone's ass. My heart was pounding and I was tense, so tense that it felt like I was going to have a heart attack or a stroke. I had sharp pains on the left side of my chest and down toward my shoulder. Troubles with the invisible wounds would cause Soldiers like me to give up on life and end up on the wrong path, like getting into drugs and self-destructive patterns that would lead them to their own death or in jail for life before they realized they needed help. Someday, hopefully I can get the help I need.

Around January 2010, early Sunday morning at one o'clock, while I was sleeping, my Squad leader decided to come by the house just to see what I was doing. I did not know why he did that, but he did, and from what I was told, he did it to the rest of the Squad as well. When I got to the door, he asked me where my phone was. I told him it was somewhere in the house. He told me that I needed to have my phone close by. I told him it was one in the morning, I wasn't worried about my phone, and I wasn't going to keep my phone strapped to my ass, waiting for him to call. I was about to have some nasty words for him, but I knew he was a Staff Sergeant and it was one o'clock in the morning and I didn't want to wake up my neighbors. He left shortly thereafter, but I was so pissed and that same anger and hatred inside me had grown so much I couldn't sleep. I didn't go to sleep until six o'clock. While I was awake, I had thoughts like, *I'm so tired of this shit*, and *I can't wait until I get out of the Army*. I did four tours to Iraq and all I wanted to do was to be left alone. No phone calls, don't come by my house—just leave me alone.

In September 2009, at Camp Marez in Iraq, I almost put my left foot in my roommate's chest because of some stupid bullshit he was tripping on. He had gone on R&R two weeks before and when I left for R&R, I thought I had a clean, soft cap. I thought I had washed it, and when I got my stuff from the laundry place, I thought my clean, soft cap was in there. I had to leave that night for R&R, and I looked in his wall locker and saw that he had a new hat, so I took it.

When I returned back from R&R, the first person that I made an effort to see was my roommate. When I saw him, I didn't even say hi or what's up. I straight up told him that I took his new hat for R&R. I told him that I was sorry for taking it, but I would buy him a brand-new one as soon as I got a chance. He said it was not a problem. Two days later, when we were in the room, he told me that he didn't like the fact that I went into his wall locker. I became extremely angry, and I yelled at the top of my lungs, "Look, motherfucker, I didn't have to tell you that I took your hat!" and I told him to shut the fuck up. I then started talking about other issues I had with him as a roommate. I told him if he didn't like it, he could get the fuck out. I was so close to putting my hands on him that I really had to find some type of grip and walk out of the room.

After that issue, I rarely stayed in the room, but if I did it was for a short time. When we were done with work, I would go to my room, take a shower, grab my weapon, and walk down to the MWR and instant message every night with my wife. I did this to keep from putting this douchebag in the hospital.

I kept the same routine until we left Iraq for good. I didn't go to the room until one in the morning and that way he'd be asleep, and all I had to do was go to sleep and get up at six to do it all over again. As you can see, I did my best to avoid trouble due to my anger and rising tension, but at the same time that was not a healthy lifestyle. I should have never had thoughts of beating my roommate's ass or have thoughts of sending him to the hospital.

When the 84th Engineers returned to normal duty day schedule after block leaves, I still found myself picking up old habits before leaving for Iraq, like getting up at four in the morning and leaving the house at 0430 and getting to Schofield at 0450. However, my anxiety was building. My heart would race like I had been running for miles, and my head would start hurting badly. I went through this every morning and when I came to formation. I was just numb as if I was there but not there. Every time the cannon went off for us to salute to the flag in the morning, it really put me back into Iraq's mood and had me think of every event that could pop up in my mind, like when mortar rounds came into Camp Anaconda or mortar rounds came in on Christmas Day in 2008 at Camp Marez in Mosul.

Therefore, the whole time we did PT, my mind wasn't on PT at all. I looked around at the sky for incoming rounds into Hamilton Field, and when it was time to run I just didn't feel like running at all. My biggest concern was that I needed help, but dealing with 84th Engineers and the way they did things, they would want you to just suck it up and drive on knowing that I just did my fourth tour, and three of them were with the 84th.

When the 84th Engineers did the SRP at Conroy's Bowl in January 2010, I hoped to get some help from the Soldier Assistance Center. I told them I had just completed four tours to Iraq and I needed help with my issues. I had finally gotten an appointment to see a counselor, but it was a very short visit because it seemed like the counselor was pressed for time. It seemed like he had bigger issues he wanted to take care of rather than help a Soldier like me who was trying to do the right thing by seeking help first. I was trying not to get myself in trouble by hurting others or hurting myself due to my PTSD. Dealing with SAC at Schofield Barracks, it seemed like they were more worried about these young Soldiers who ranged from E-1 through E-4, who were trying to play crazy. They tried to play crazy because they got word that their unit was heading to Iraq or Afghanistan. So getting an appointment at SAC was thirty days out, and I needed to be seen weekly.

I only had two appointments with SAC, and I told them I needed more help, so they referred me to a military source I didn't know, but they did outsource me to see a counselor out in Ewa Beach. I did eight sessions with her and she gave me a written statement of her conclusion that I was suffering from Post-Traumatic Stress Disorder (PTSD). I took the written letter to Military OneSource and hoped to get treated or be seen more. The letter sat at Military OneSource for two weeks until I finally went there to find out what the delay was all about.

The Things That Help Me Keep My Mind Off of PTSD Issues

After no support with SAC and no further guidance from Military OneSource, a special project had come down for a fellow NCO, me, and another Soldier to go to Fort Shafter to work with a Sergeant Major over in G3 at 8th TSC. I was happy to get away from Schofield and my unit because I wasn't getting any help with my issues. When I was with my unit, I was constantly on edge and irritated by other Soldiers, and I found myself calling them nasty names when they showed up late to formation. I would say things like, "Mother fucker, if you can't come to work on time, don't even bother to show up for work because I don't have time for Soldiers who don't take their career seriously and can't come to work on time." It was an everyday thing with me when I dealt with Soldiers like that. However, as an NCO, I shouldn't have been like that toward Soldiers.

As time went by, the next thing that was going to happen would be me putting my hands on those Soldiers. I'd end up in trouble and Soldiers would have been in the hospital due to my anger and short temper with them. I was the same way with NCOs and Officers who were higher ranking than me. The three of us started out building simple walls with sheet rock, mud, tape, and paint. When the Sergeant Major saw our work, he was happy and wanted to keep us. Somehow between 84th Engineers and 8th TSC, they worked out some type of "drug deal," and we stayed doing special projects all the way until my enlistment contract date was up on December 20, 2010, which meant I didn't get seen again by SAC and there was no support from my unit, the 643rd 84th Engineer Battalion. During the entire year of 2010, while working for the Sergeant Major, my chain of command never came down to check on the three of us personnel nor did they ever come down to see some of our work. The distance of travel from Schofield to Shafter was only sixteen miles, but they would fly from Honolulu, Hawaii, to Thailand and check on those Soldiers. The things that we did for 8th TSC were:

1. Building five flag boxes for an outdoor ceremony, during which 9th MSC always borrowed the flag boxes from 8th TSC
2. Doing various finish and carpentry work and building other flag boxes for units like 45th Quartermaster
3. Building G6 a customer service area
4. Building G3 a conference room
5. Completing random projects for Command Sergeant Major of the 8th TSC
6. Conducting building repair services, such as air conditioning and carpet repairs

We all enjoyed working for Sergeant Major. He understood I had PTSD and the projects he had us doing kept my short temper and anger at bay. When I had bad nightmares, it was three in the morning, and I couldn't sleep, I would just get up and head over to Shafter Flats to the motor pool and start working on one of the projects we were working on. When my fellow Soldiers would show up at 0730 and see that some of the work was done, they thought I was pretty fast. Really I was going in so early because I had bad nightmares, and I helped get projects done ahead of schedule. Sergeant Major thought we were the best Engineer Soldiers ever, but again, he never knew that I was coming into the motor pool at three in the morning. Even though I was still doing good work for Sergeant Major, I did have my moments and I said some mean words to another NCO who was working for the Command Sergeant Major. Luckily, Command Sergeant Major was on vacation, but I told him that if he didn't like what I did, I could just pack up all of my tools and go home for the day. Or better yet, I would go home and I wouldn't come back until everyone pulled their heads out of their asses.

I also had another outburst with two personnel at Home Depot about their lack of quality customer service toward Soldiers. I had some nasty words for those employees and the sad part is that I was in my US Army uniform, knowing that I should always show professional behavior when I was in uniform.

That day was really bad for me. My fellow NCO, who had known me for two years, had never seen me so pissed off before. He told me he hoped he'd never piss me off. He knew I needed help, but no one at SAC or my unit would help me. He also said that no one would get off their asses to get me some help unless I hurt myself or someone else, but by then it would be too late because I would be in jail and someone would be killed because of my outburst. However, I was trying my best to do the right thing and fight to get some help.

Dealing with My Issues at 9th TSG

I went to 9th TSG in January of 2011, holding a 12H slot (Construction Supervisor), hoping that it would be a change of pace and that some of my issues would go away. When we had Soldier Readiness Processing (SRP) in March 2011, I did fill out some paper work that would help me get some help with my PTSD and finally, months later, I started to get help.

During those months, however, I was doing some projects for my first-line supervisor. He thought of me as a very good NCO who came to work on time, sometimes even two hours before the workday, and started to get things going for the day. Most of my duties were installing new sinks and faucets in Building 1554. I remodeled two classrooms in the same building and laid new floors. During those times, everyone looked at me as a hardworking NCO, but the real deal was that I was doing my best to stay busy every minute of the day and not think about my issues stemming from PTSD. I completed other projects as well, but when all the special projects were over, or we had run out of money due to short budgets, there was no more work for me. By then, I saw that depression had set in along with my other issues, and I started to have my inner rage develop. I had to fight really hard not to go off on someone who was higher ranking than me. For example, I was tired of seeing reserve Soldiers who were in the same rank as me or higher, like a Master Sergeant or a Full Bird Colonel, who never deployed to Iraq or Afghanistan. And here I was with four tours to Iraq, I had more than one combat patch, and these Soldiers didn't have one. The saddest thing was that these Soldiers sat behind a desk looking at a computer screen all day every day collecting a paycheck as if they were doing some real work, when they really were just taking up space. How did they get on the AGR program (Active Guard Reserves)? Soldiers like me should have been the first to get picked up for AGR but never did. Yet I did all that shit in Iraq, and I had been through a lot of stuff over there in six years. In fact, I put in more work in those six years than the average Soldier who did twenty years in service and never spent a day in danger, but at the same time they were supposed to be our leaders of tomorrow. Last time I checked, leaders lead from the front, not the rear, and we had these Senior NCOs and Officers walking around with no combat patch. This meant they had never been to Iraq or Afghanistan, while there were NCOs (E-5 Sergeants) like me who had been there and done that four different times.

If you ask me, there's something wrong with the Army system if these so-called leaders could find loopholes to get around the system so they wouldn't have to deploy to Iraq or Afghanistan. The sad thing was that I had to see this every day or every time I had weekend drills. When I was on active duty, it really made my heart burn as if it was on fire, and at times, I thought a heart attack was coming. I tried to avoid them at all costs because I didn't want to hear anything of what they had to say about the Army. Situations like this caused a Soldier like me to be a walking time bomb, which meant that I could go off on somebody regardless what rank they were and would care less about what happened afterward.

Trip to American Samoa with PTSD

American Samoa was a place for me to deal with my issues. It was my second visit in March 2012 and all my memories and flashbacks didn't hit me at all. For the first time, I felt like I had the real me back—I mean the real me before 9/11. In American Samoa, there wasn't anything on that island that reminded me of Iraq. For an example, Kunia Road in Hawaii reminded me of a road in Iraq up in Mosul just past the bridge leaving downtown.

Anyway, I worked for a Major who was my old boss at 9th TSG, and he knew my capabilities on how I got things done as a 12H Construction Supervisor. He had seen what I had done as far as building repairs and other projects, and he was aware of my PTSD issues.

In March 2012, the Major requested that I come out to do some work for him, so my chain of command allowed me to do my annual training in American Samoa to get some work done at the reserve center. My job consisted of laying new flooring and installing new sinks, which didn't happen due to lack of material on the island, but I did lay 2,500 square feet of tiles for the Major. Now, as a 12 Hotel, your job is not laying floors. The United States Army is not in the business of teaching Soldiers how to lay floors; it was just that I learned how to lay floors back when I was twenty-two and I was in a trade school called Clearfield Job Corp in Utah, long before I joined the Army. However, the Major had seen some flooring jobs I'd done for him when he was my boss at Fort Shafter down in Building 1554 in Rooms 106 and 107. After laying the tile in American Samoa at the reserve center, I was able to teach some of the Soldiers who were working under me the tricks of the trade of floor covering. Some had taken to learning how to lay floors so well that they wanted to lay floors in their own houses. By then, I felt like a true NCO, I had the knowledge to do a lot of things as a Construction Engineer, and I was able to teach Soldiers some of the skills I had. Laying floors wasn't easy and could be really hard on one's back, knees, and hips, but the finished product was worth the pain. Luckily, I was able to go back to the hotel and soak in the hot tub or a hot bubble bath. My issue with PTSD was so far away from me while I was in American Samoa that it felt like it left my soul.

One Saturday morning, I was in a town called Leone. The town of Leone was hit with the tsunami back in 2009 and the damage remains to this day. I saw this family building a wall using CMU blocks. I stopped and talked to the father and son for a bit, and I decided to help them. I helped them get ahead of their schedule. They asked where I learned how to lay block. I told them I did it when I was on active duty in the Army, and I told them how I laid block out in the Marshall Islands back in 1998 and 2000.

Later that day, we had to go back to the store to get more materials, and the son stopped me and told me he wanted to get his mom a new washing machine. I told him that it was cool but what he really wanted to know is if I could put it in for him. I said I would help him get the washing machine in the house. Well, he bought the washing machine, we loaded up in the truck, and headed back to Leone. When we got back to the house, the son and I got the washing machine into the house and put it where he wanted. I asked him where the old washing machine was, and he said that there was not one; this was the first washing machine in this house. I said to myself, *Oh my God, this man bought a washing machine, but the house has no water line going to the washing machine or even a drain line for the washing machine.* He was so happy that he bought a washing machine for his mom, and his mom who was very sick at the time was very happy too. I had to break the bad news to him to tell him that the washing machine was not going to work at all without any water line or drain line to the washing machine. I told him that next Saturday we would go back to Ace Hardware together to get new drain pipes and water lines. On that Saturday, we had got everything we needed to get the job done and by Saturday evening, the washing machine was in operation. The son was so happy that he couldn't believe he met me by me stopping and talking to them. He said he had Samoan friends on the island and no one ever came out to help him the way I did. I felt really good to know that I was able to help someone in need after the tsunami hit in 2009. I always wanted to go to American Samoa to help out when the tsunami hit, but I never thought I would be able to go out there. I think between the Major and the family I helped, my PTSD improved. It seemed like I put my issues and problems aside, started helping others, and they both kept me busy throughout the ten days I was in American Samoa, and I loved every minute of it.

The flooring project with the Major was done a day ahead of schedule. The Major and his staff were very happy and really amazed at the skills I had. I made a joke with them about my skills and told them that when they see me, I was more than just an E-5 Sergeant; I was a NCO with many skills and talents. The Major wanted me to come back and do some more work for him; I was looking forward to getting some stuff done. American Samoa was high maintenance due to its location. I thought going to places like American Samoa and other places would keep my PTSD further and further away from me, but I learned from being in the Reserves for a little bit over a year that whoever has control of the budget acts like it is their own money and would be the first to say, "We don't have any funds to send you anywhere." But a week later, ten other people would be going somewhere.

It seemed like in the Reserves when they needed things to be done but they really didn't want to do it, they would take a maintenance problem and say they needed funds to fix the problem. When they got the money, they would take the funds and spend it on something else. For example, if five people needed to go to Guam, then those people would go. Meanwhile, the maintenance problem would still be there and I stayed put, willing to get the problem solved. They should have just bought the part or whatever instead of getting the contractor to do the same job that I could do. That was another reason why funding kept going out the window. Meanwhile,

I sat at 9th TSG, letting my PTSD issues build up and allowing a good chance for me to blow up at someone. By then, I would get noticed and people thought I was crazy needing some help, when all they needed to do was stop treating the budget like their own money and allow me to do my job.

When I was able to do my job as a Facility Maintenance Supervisor conducting maintenance duties, I didn't have time to bother with Soldiers higher ranking than then me who didn't have a combat patch, or civilians who had "GS jobs," government status jobs, sitting on their asses all day looking at a computer screen and talking about how they couldn't get their jobs done, or they would put the blame on someone for the reason why they couldn't get their job done. Basically, I was tired of the piss poor work ethics and lack of teamwork.

With my job, it showed if I got the job done or not. For instance, if a toilet had a leak when it was flushed, it would be my job to fix it, and it showed that I fixed it because there were no leaks. I hoped things would change because I could not stand to be around the 9th TSG with nothing to do.

I was so close to having some nasty words with a civilian who worked in my section. Every time I came in, he would say, "Hey, I have this work order here and the toilet is clogged. Can you fix it?" The funny thing was that I was in civilian clothes, and all I wanted to do was turn in a paper that my Master Sergeant wanted from me. I could not understand how this man thought he was the boss of me, but he would catch hell from me if he didn't get off his ass and do some work. Better yet, he should not have been speaking to me at all because he was not my boss; the only bosses I had were Sergeant First Class E-7, Master Sergeant E-8, Lieutenant Colonel (LT. COL) and Major. Those were my bosses. This was the same civilian who called SFC knowing that SFC (E-7) and I were working on a big job at Building 1558, that our Lieutenant Colonel wanted us to change out the warehouse lights and install brighter lights in the combative area. This civilian called the SFC and informed him that the urinals were clogged in Building 1557 on the first and second floors. SFC informed him that we were busy and it would be a while before we could look at it. The call came in at 0800 hours on a Friday, and around 1415 hours the same day, I needed to go to the offices to get something signed before they went home for the day.

When I went into the office, that civilian again was sitting on his ass, looking at the computer screen, and my other first-line supervisor hit me up saying that the urinals were clogged and asked if I could take a look at it. I said okay but that I had come to the office for something else, and the SFC I was working with still needed me at the warehouse. I went to look and both urinals were clogged. I went back to the office, looked in our little toolbox, grabbed a flathead screwdriver, tape, and blank sheet of printing paper. I went back to the bathroom and used the flathead screwdriver to turn off the water at the urinal, then took the tape, sectioned it off, and wrote on the blank sheet of paper: "out of order" on both urinals on the first and second floor. It took me a whole five minutes and that civilian had called SFC at eight in the morning, which meant the urinals had been overflowing for six fucking hours when it took me a whole five minutes to do what I did. All this while that civilian guy sat on his ass looking at a computer screen all fucking day or, better yet, shining the seat with this ass like Congress does in Washington.

It let me know that the actual GS employees thought it would take an act of Congress to get them fired. Meanwhile, I worked my ass off with an organization that didn't have any teamwork ethic or the idea of "hey, let's get this shit done," and I was struggling to keep my PTSD out of me. There were times were I had been so frustrated with the piss-poor work ethic in the 9th TSG that I just got up and walked to my truck and went home for the day. I did not care if it was ten in the morning, I would go home for the day. Now I understand how someone can just get a shotgun or whatever and just start shooting up the place, and people would be wondering what was wrong or saying, "Oh shit, Sergeant Duckworth has gone crazy!" By then it would be too late because I'd be heading to jail, but I really understand how people can go off in the deep end, especially with Soldiers like me with PTSD. So far, from what I've seen since I've been out of active duty, is that there is no place in the United States for fellow Soldiers like me with PTSD, and I'm a damn good Construction Engineer Soldier. It was as if no one wanted to hire me because I had way too much experience, or since they knew I had been to Iraq one too many times they thought that something was wrong with me. Well there was, but I was trying to work through it and have a normal life like everyone else. The bottom line is no one will give you the time of day.

When I was in my group session at the VA for my PTSD, there were a few guys there from the Vietnam War era, and I thought that it was odd to see them in my group session. However, between the Vietnam War, Iraq, and Afghanistan, we all had two things in common: we were Soldiers who struggled with PTSD. One of the Vietnam Vets told us a story about how he was an E-7 helicopter mechanic for the Black Hawks on the Medevac side, and at that time he understood how the pilot of the Medevac chopper unit got all the credit for going into a hot zone in hostile fire and picking up the wounded Soldiers. When the pilot returned, he would get all the glory for saving the Soldiers or bringing back wounded Soldiers. The Vietnam Vet understood that part, but what he didn't understand was that no one looked at the helicopter mechanic who kept up with the maintenance on the Medevac choppers. He also said that when he completed his twenty years of service, he applied for every helicopter mechanic position on the island, but no one would give him the time of day. At that time, I did feel sorry for him, but today I truly feel his pain—it has really hit me hard for the past three months or so. Like for me, I did four tours to Iraq from January 2003 to November 2009, and I was a Construction Engineer who built things all over Iraq and conducted thousands of miles of road repairs after an IED went off. I know I put my heart and soul in the war in Iraq, scared or not, but the bottom line was to get the job done.

In 2003, I installed two hundred miles of pipeline for fuel and in 2004 and 2006, we built Camp LSA Anaconda with living quarters for our fellow Soldiers, and we poured over two hundred thousand cubic yards of concrete at the airstrip just so that each Chinook could have its own landing pad. From 2008 to 2009, I was stationed at Camp Marez in Mosul where we built a total of forty-two sea huts throughout various camps in Iraq and conducted road repair missions. So again, I understand how that Vietnam Vet felt about getting a job. You go through so much shit during wartime, and at the end of your day you still got the job done. Keep in mind: this was after working fifteen-hour days with no time off. When you complete your service with the military and try to apply for jobs that you know your skills fit but no one will give you the time of day, it's frustrating. You have great skills and talent but nowhere to take it. Listen to the words in *Rambo: First Blood* at the end while the character Rambo is having his meltdown with Colonel Trautman. He says in Vietnam he could fly gunships, drive tanks, and was in charge of million-dollar equipment, but back in the real world he couldn't even get a job parking cars. If you sit back and think about it, Rambo's statement was made back in 1982, but it's the same problem today. Our so-called government has turned the other cheek and acts as if these problems finding work don't exist. Like I said earlier, there is no place for Soldiers who have the hard-work attitude, are well trained, and have a broad range of experience. No one will give you the time of day if you have PTSD. If you ever watch any of the *Rambo* movies, he never came home from Vietnam; he was always stuck in Thailand doing some small work for the monks. I understand why he never came home until after the fourth movie. If you look at the ending of that movie, he walked on a country road and on a long driveway out in the country. To tell you the truth, I believe Soldiers like me need to be out in the country with no one around. PTSD is a very bad mental and emotional illness and anything can set you off. It might take hours or even days for you to calm down or, at times, you won't ever calm down, and the next thing you know you're only getting three hours of sleep a night. To make matters worse is it hard to sleep due to the nightmares about the war.

Looking for Work with PTSD

When Soldiers like me go through ACAP, we spend about two weeks learning about companies that love to hire qualified Soldiers, but from what I have seen, they don't. ACAP stands for Army Career and Alumni Program. It is a transition phase from military to civilian life that is supposed to help you prepare for civilian life. They talk about how much companies love to hire military, and they also teach you to write a good resume. Well, I already had a resume so I had an ACAP employee look at it to see if I needed to make any changes. She said that it looked really nice with all the right information on it, but there was one problem: on my resume, it stated that I worked on the weekends doing home remodeling on single-family homes and condos. She told me that I shouldn't put that on my resume even though it was my past experience on top of conducting the construction missions on all four tours to Iraq as well as each time I came home. I told her I worked on the weekends doing side jobs, which helped keep the PTSD from coming to the surface. She still insisted that I shouldn't put that on there because the jobs I had done on the weekend were under the table. I got very pissed off at her. I told her that she and any other company should see that I can get the jobs done when it comes to home remodeling, and they should also see that I'm a self-starter. If I'm hired to remodel a crack house, then I should be able to get it done from start to finish and have it looking like a million-dollar home. I'm able to look at a project like home remodeling and see what's needed as far as materials and get the cost estimate on how much materials will be. That is something that the United States Army teaches you when you're a Construction Engineer. I learned to transfer the construction skills I had gained while enlisted in United States Army to do side jobs. The lady overlooked the fact that I did these side jobs because I was running away from my issues like PTSD and depression. It just so happened that I did a little work on the side during the weekends, when I could have started drinking, doing drugs, getting into trouble with the law, or, worst case, beating up on my wife and daughter and taking my troubles out on them. But I never did; I took my troubles out on remodeling single-family homes and condos. The people for whom I did work really loved what I did to their homes and that made me want to do more.

It seemed like I was self-medicating by working on these houses and condos since I couldn't get any medical attention from SAC at Schofield Barracks. You have to understand that ever since my first tour to Iraq (January 2003 to November 2009), when I went home, I ended up doing a side job every weekend and still showed up for work for the Army every Monday through Friday. I did what I had to do to keep the PTSD issues away and spent my weekends running away from the invisible wound that no one would help me with.

When I was officially out of the Army, I applied for unemployment. Doing that was a hot mess. I always figured a group of people who had a job title were at their jobs, doing what they were getting paid to do, just like the US Army paid me to do the job I was paid to do. It took me a month to get my first check and at the same time, I was waiting for my very last paycheck from the Army. When I tried to find out what was the hold up for my first check from the unemployment office, it was like waiting for Congress to come out of recess. Somehow one piece of paper was supposed to go two doors down and have it signed by this one person, and no one ever informed me, while at the same time bills were piling up and the food pantry was getting empty. Every night I worried how I was going to pay the bills and when someone was going to hire me. I was willing to work anywhere and everywhere; I even applied for a carpentry job way out in the Arctic Circle. I figured that if someone had seen my resume—which showed that I had fourteen years of experience as a Construction Engineer, had completed four tours to Iraq conducting construction missions, and had my own United States passport, along with security clearance—my phone would be ringing off the hook with people asking me when I would be able to start work.

Things had gotten so bad with me being out of work that at night I would go through this deep depression, and there was no other help with my PTSD. I'd gotten to the point where I was outside on my bench sitting and looking out as if I was posting guard like a tower guard at Camp Anaconda, Iraq; the only thing I was missing was my M4 or my M16. I would stand there looking at the parking lot at our condo, looking for unknown people because I felt like everyone was out to fuck me over. In other words, if anyone couldn't help me and my situation and help me to not become a homeless Veteran, then I assumed they were a threat to me, so basically I didn't trust one motherfucker. I couldn't trust people to do their jobs right to keep me from being a homeless Veteran.

While I waited for my last check from the Army, one Friday evening the repo man came to my house asking for my car (a 1993 Honda accord), which I bought used because I had to send my other car to the junkyard. I only owed $1,600 so when the repo man came to my house I was so shocked and upset that my skin felt as if it was on fire. I told the repo man I was waiting for my last check and the unemployment office couldn't do their jobs right in order for me to receive my check to continue the payments on the Honda. He wanted the car and I told him that I wouldn't give it to him. He asked me where the car was and I told him, "What makes you think I will tell you where the car is?"

Later, I told him that I would have the car at my house the next day at 3:30 p.m. By then I felt like an outcast, like people didn't even care what I had done for this country and what I had gone through after serving four tours to Iraq. I felt so much hatred toward civilians living here in this free country called the United States. It's the same United States that my fellow Soldiers and I had fought for and some of my fellow Soldiers had died for—to protect our way of life. Here were people like me with major issues going on, who didn't get any support from any organization with medical help or guidance with PTSD. Self-medicating wasn't working unless I wanted to do drugs and drink and get in to trouble with the law. Maybe then I would get some attention after a criminal case and find out that I had not been mentally stable, but by then it would be too late. Luckily, I'm not into drugs and I do my best to obey the laws, but it is a constant battle dealing with the civilian way of life after spending six years running back and forth to Iraq.

I had been home for two years and still struggled with everyday normal life. In the month of November, my body was geared up to go to Iraq, and it was really hard for me to get into the Christmas mood. The reason for it was because I was in Mosul, Iraq, on December 25, 2008, and I had been bombed on at Camp Marez all night long, in full gear.

At this point in my life, I just wanted to go back to Iraq where things made sense to me. Over there, I had been shot at and came close to having my body parts all over the desert from IED explosions on the side of the road, not to mention mortar rounds coming toward me. At least I knew where I stood over there, but here in the United States, where I was born and raised, I felt that there was no support for fellow Soldiers as far as getting help and getting a better paying job, where I could make enough money to pay both mortgages, put food on the table, and be able to do things with my family. Shit, it almost made me believe that illegal immigrants got more support and other government benefits, not to mention jobs, when they snuck over to the United States. When American Soldiers come home from war, we get treated like third-class citizens. Explain to me why we have more homeless Veterans on our streets than we do illegal immigrants? Please tell me. Don't worry, I'll wait...

The repo man never got my car from me. I went to the bank to talk to someone about what I needed to do to get the repo man off my ass. They told me that I needed to come up with $850 by that Saturday. It was 5:30 p.m. on a Friday, so my wife had to use her paycheck and dig into our little accounts that had $200 here and $300 there and dig for some lose money around the house. When Saturday came, we gave them the $850 and told them to get the repo man off our asses. I did mention to them the reason for the holdup was that I was waiting for my last check from the Army and I would pay the car off. When the repo man came back to the house at 3:30 p.m. that Saturday, I was being a smart ass with him and told him that I wasn't giving him the car because it was not there, and I went and paid it up. When I said that, the repo man looked at me as if I wasn't supposed to pay it up to where it would be current. It looked like he was mad because he knew he wasn't going to get his commission check from the bank that day.

Monday morning, I went up to Schofield Barracks to see the finance department. When you go in, you're supposed to sign in and wait your turn. Well, I didn't do that. I asked the Sergeant First Class why it was taking so long to get my last check from the Army. When I asked her, I wasn't very nice, and it was at the point where if she wanted to, she could have called the Military Police to get me out of there. I told her the reason I was so upset was because the repo man was at my house on Friday evening, waiting to take my car over $1,600. I told her that if they would have repossessed it, how was I supposed to look for a job without a car? I asked her if that's what she did to Soldiers who had done four tours to Iraq and decided to get out of the Army after fourteen years of service. I said, "Now you want to hold their money up as if it is your money?" After all that was said, she started to do her job and researched the issue for me. Later, I got a call from her saying that my money would be in my account in twenty-four to forty-eight hours. It was a darn shame that I had to go there and raise hell, have my chest on fire, and display rage to get the money that was owed to me. If you sit back and think about it, this is how people end up walking into a building and start shooting the place up and then asking where their money is.

Another thing is, you don't know what state of mind a Soldier is in. In today's world, people look at PTSD as someone who is heavy into drugs and alcohol, getting in trouble with the law, and beating up family members. If you want to know what my state of mind is with dealing with getting a job and dealing with my PTSD issues and everything that comes along with it, just watch the movie, *For Colored Girls*. An actor named Michael Ealy plays a return Soldier from Iraq who tries to find work and deal with the VA about getting help with his issues. He has a girlfriend with two kids who tries to help him with his issues, but she can only do so much. The movie shows how I feel every day. The only difference is that I never threw my kids out the third-story window, and I generally don't drink, but I do have a few drinks occasionally just so I can make it through and write about my issues with PTSD. So if Soldiers like me don't get help, bad things will happen and it is only a matter of time. But by then it is too late.

Getting Fired from a Civilian Job Due to PTSD

After getting out of the Army, it took me about seven months to get a job. I wasn't too familiar with this job, which was a warehouse position. Damn, I had done so much stuff for this country and the American people would not even give me the time of day. Not to mention, I still owned two properties (one in Hawaii and one in Lawton, Oklahoma), which I ended up losing later due to not having a job and accepting a lower wage of $16.00 an hour as a warehouse tech. In the Army, I made way more when you add my E-5 base pay, BAH, COLA. I believed I was wrongfully terminated of employment as a warehouse technician on 06 January 2012, after being employed with the company since 20 July, 2011.

On my employee performance review form that was filled out by the warehouse supervisor, it stated that it seemed like my mind and career were somewhere else, which caused me to lose focus on the primary department and duties. The warehouse manager didn't bring that to my attention until the day of my termination of employment. I had never been written up for it, and the warehouse manager was aware of my PTSD issues. He was aware that I was seeing a counselor at Tripler Medical Center. I felt like I was being discriminated against due to seeking treatment and my mental disability ever since I had an appointment with the counselor on 03 December 2011 and gave him an update on what was going on with my treatment, as he instructed me to do, and briefed the warehouse manager on what PTSD is and how it occurs.

My employment performance review form was created on 12 December 2011 and I didn't see the form until 06 January 2012, my last day of my employment. I went to work at five in the morning and was fired by 7:30 a.m. In the statement, it also stated that I continued to make mistakes that hindered the department and caused others to invest time into correcting the errors. The warehouse manager had never written me up for any of the mistakes that I may have made. Furthermore, if I made major mistakes, why would the warehouse manager allow me to come in at five o'clock in the morning and get off at five o'clock in the evening when my work schedule was 10:00 to 6:30, Monday through Friday? I had also worked a few Saturdays when the manager asked me to. I had been coming into work early ever since September when I was fired. My two coworkers didn't know I was making errors, and if they knew I was making errors, they should have made sure that I would make the corrections and see to it that it wouldn't happen again. The three of us worked really well together, and we had become really close during the five months I worked with them. One woman was really in tears when she found out I was being fired. After leaving the Army, it took me seven months to get a job and five months to get fired from a job in which I had no experience.

Prior to being employed as a warehouse technician, I applied for a Com-Tech position that fit my background and experience. I completed the online application and submitted the DD214, my resume, and my last NCO Evaluation Report. When I got called to do the interview for the Com-Tech position, the supervisor who interviewed me had seen my documents and my background experience in construction and home remodeling. Somehow, the interview went from a Com-Tech interview to a warehouse interview, knowing that I didn't have any warehouse experience. I ended up having the interview with the warehouse manager. I told the warehouse manager that I didn't have any warehouse experience and that my background was in construction engineering and home remodeling. About two weeks later, I ended up being hired as a warehouse technician. I got two weeks' training in warehouse daily duties and as time went on, I thought I was doing pretty well until the day of my termination.

During the time I was working as a warehouse technician, I did apply for another position as a service tech and a field supervisor, but

I didn't get either position. I did get an interview for the field supervisor and was interviewed by a supervisor. He told me in the interview that he saw that I had fourteen years of experience in construction in the Army, but I didn't have any experience in home repairs. I told him to look two lines down on my resume and he would see that I did home remodeling on the island. They thought I worked for another company or a subcontractor, and I told him that I worked for the Army Monday through Friday, and on the weekends I did my own side jobs. I explained that I did these jobs because someone had heard of me or seen my work and wanted their house done. I also stated that I was a maintenance supervisor at my Reserve Unit at 9th TSG and maintained buildings on Fort Shafter, American Samoa, Guam, and Alaska. It seemed that all the information I gave them had gone in one ear and out the other.

The next day I e-mailed some pictures of home remodeling to the warehouse supervisor and the other field supervisor, and all I got was a response that I had done a nice job. The warehouse manager did say that he thought I didn't belong in the warehouse and that I did have some skills, but it wasn't important to them. They still continued to hire new technicians, knowing that I was working in the warehouse, doing a job I didn't have any experience with. Not to mention, I was an Iraq Veteran.

At the same time, this company had a contract with the Army at Schofield Barracks to maintain the housing on that base. On 09 January 2012, I had gotten a call from a human resource manager to inform me they had a position for me since I was lacking some experience in the warehouse. The position was as a Preventive Maintenance Tech making $12.00 an hour. When I was the warehouse tech, I started out at $16.00 an hour with no experience. I told them I had to think about it, but to tell you the truth, it was really a slap in the face four different times: one was for not moving me when I was an employee; two, I didn't get the field supervisor position; three, they called me three days after they fired me and wanted me to start at $12.00 an hour; and four, they didn't give me an interview when I applied for the service tech position while I was working in the warehouse, but they still continued to hire technicians. I hoped something could be done about this because if they can mistreat me like they did, that meant they would do the same thing to another Veteran who had completed their service with the Army and tried to get a job that fit the job background they had in the military.

When I got fired that Friday, everything that had happened that day didn't really sink in until Friday evening. My wife was upset for what they had done, and she was surprised that I took it so well. But at the time, I didn't have any choice but to be the bigger person and walk away. My thought was to get back at the managers who all signed the evaluation paperwork agreed to fire me—those managers need to count their blessings and enjoy the same air that I'm breathing. That Friday night, I hated to see my wife in tears because I lost my job. She asked me, the man of the house, "What are we going to do?"

For the first time, I didn't have any answers. Yes, I was frustrated and had tons of hatred in me. My first thought was to take my anger out on my wife, but I didn't. My second thought was to find the warehouse manager who fired me—I knew where his part-time job was. I had thoughts of driving down there with my twenty-two-ounce east-wing framing hammer and beating his brains in so he would have his life turned upside down, or killing him. I was truly ready to drive down there after watching my wife cry, knowing I couldn't do anything about it. So I got up, didn't say a word, and left the house with my hammer. Yes, I headed toward his part-time job, but one hundred things ran through my head. I was enraged and it felt as if my heart was burning and my skin was on fire. I ended up heading toward the freeway away from his part-time job, Home Depot, and went to Tripler. I was planning to turn myself into the mental ward and say, "Please help me before I hurt someone."

When I got to Tripler and parked in the parking lot by the emergency room, I sat in the truck for ten minutes and thought that these people at Tripler couldn't help me. So I started up the truck and was about to head back home, but my mind was so frustrated about things that I couldn't see my way out of the parking lot. The parking lot was empty and it was dark. I ended up being in the parking lot of a baseball field at Tripler, which was a safe place for me. It was dark and no one was around me. My anger and rage was so out of control that I was glad my wife wasn't with me. She was texting me wondering what I was doing and where I was, but I never returned her texts. I walked around the baseball field for three hours being frustrated about what had happened that day and not understanding how things worked in the civilian world. But I was a Soldier who had never been in this type of trouble. I mean I did my job well in the Army, and I was involved in construction projects all over the world. It looked like this was the thanks I got for serving my country. At that point, I really didn't know what to do at all; this would be the time where most people would have just started doing drugs or, better yet, just started selling drugs. After all, you have no job, bills are piling up, and you have a wife at home in distress. That day was so bad for me, I wanted to drop everything and just go back to Iraq. At least there, I could never get fired. I did my job well under harsh conditions and bills got paid. I was doing all of that while my life was on the line every minute of the day in Iraq, which told me that I was only good enough to have a job unless my life was on the line. I was at the baseball park for at least three or four hours before I went home.

During the time I was at the baseball field, I came to the conclusion that I really did not trust people; I mean if you tell your manager that you have a drinking problem and you're seeking counseling, there shouldn't be any backlash because you're getting help. I believe that this is what happened when I put too much trust in supervisors, thinking there would be some type of caring for the employees, but there was not. So again, it was hard for me to trust people, and it was hard for me to trust banks. It had been two years that I had not made any mortgage payments on any of my houses due to me not having a job or making enough to maintain my two homes that I worked so hard for. How can you when you have supervisors like the warehouse manager fire you because you have PTSD but you're trying to live like a normal person and seek help? It seemed like I was being punished for seeking help and developing PTSD while fighting for my country. This is the part where Soldiers would say, "Fuck it, I give up," and end up doing things that cause them to be in trouble with the law or, worse, commit suicide.

So like I said before, it was hard for me to trust banks, banks that were supposed to help you with your home loan. While I waited for my back pay to be in from the VA, I was behind $12,000 on my mortgages for my house in Oklahoma. When my back pay came in, I called the bank and asked them if they would work with me because my back pay was $8,000. They said yes and I asked them to mail me a letter stating what they would do for me if I sent them $8,000. I left for American Samoa for ten days to work on facility maintenance at the Army Reserve building and when I came home, there was no letter.

Two weeks went by and I heard a knock on the door. I was being served court papers from Tulsa, Oklahoma, for the foreclosure hearing for my house. I was so hurt I said, "Fuck this shit." I was so hurt and discouraged about how banks and other loan companies didn't care about Soldiers, especially the Soldiers who fought in Iraq and Afghanistan. Meanwhile, these loan companies and banks were making billions while our Soldiers were out fighting to protect America's freedom and its way of life.

When Soldiers come home, they don't get any help or support from the people for whom we fought. This tells me when I got out of active duty, I could start a career as a drug dealer on the street and make the money just to pay my mortgage payments on both of my homes on time during the year of 2011. The banks would never ask where I got the money from; they would just be happy that they were getting the payments on time. That's how all banks are: you can miss two payments on your loan, and they don't care how you come up with the full amount; they won't ask where the money comes from.

Separation from Wife and Daughter

My wife and I decided that she would leave the island and take our daughter so I could focus on getting help for my PTSD. It became clear that we were one step away from being homeless. After active duty service, I couldn't make the house payment at all. One day back in June 2012, my wife texted me and asked if she should send a resume out to Hill Air Force Base for a job and I said yes. We were both thinking that she would send out a resume but no one would respond back, especially after I sent tons of resumes out and I didn't get a response. Well, she sent it out on a Thursday and her cell phone rang off the hook early Friday morning Hawaii time. The manager called her and wanted to do a Skype interview with her the following Friday. The interview went well and they gave my wife until August 15 to report to work. Luckily, I was on orders and I used that time to get the car ready to be shipped to California. I even got new brakes put on the car, as well as new tires and an oil change.

While I did those things, it put me in the mood of thinking I was going on a convoy, making sure that the car was ready for travel when it arrived to California. My wife paid for plane tickets and a hotel. When they arrived in Oakland, California, my cousin met my family for the first time and took my wife to the carport to get the car. Since my wife was stuck on the island since 2004, and they were now in Oakland, they wanted to take a mini vacation trip to San Francisco and visit Pier 39 and Fisherman's Wharf. It was nice they had that opportunity. My wife, daughter, and mother-in-law made it to Utah. It was truly a home for them. My wife said that it was the best choice we ever made, to come back to Utah with family and friends. I wanted to drop everything in Hawaii and just leave with the shirt on my back, but I didn't want to give the Army the satisfaction. The

United States Army owed me medical care for my PTSD and other medical issues, and possibly an early retirement.

During my first week home, I felt very alone. When I had left for Iraq four different times, I didn't feel so alone. I left my family knowing that I had a serious job to do over there and had to fight twice as hard to come home all in one piece. But this time when my family left and I was home alone, it made me understand how my wife felt when I left for Iraq. I asked my daughter (age twelve) if she missed me, and she said, "No Daddy, I don't."

I asked why and she said that it was just like I was in Iraq and that I would be coming home soon. It was a good way to look at it from a twelve-year-old's perspective, but at the same time it lets me know that that was what she saw her daddy as. She saw her daddy in the Army in uniform, he'd come home, and the next year he would be gone again for another year, and that was how her childhood had been. After all, she was two years old during 9/11, and in 2002, I spent the whole year training with my unit (Bravo Company 62nd Engineers, Fort Sill, Oklahoma). In January 2003, we left for Iraq, so from January 2003 to November 2009, I ran back and forth to Iraq, missing my daughter growing up. It was hard to make up for lost time, so I tried to hit the beach as much as I could with my family. My daughter loves the water and loves to swim a lot. Once she was in the water, it was hard to get her out. We swam to look at fish in the water sometimes, and we also went snorkeling. For those small moments, I didn't think about events that occurred in Iraq, but I still stayed hypervigilant, making sure that people in the water were not in any danger. That is a constant battle every day: being hypervigilant. Sometimes, it keeps me in the house for two weeks at a time because I don't want to leave the house and see stupid shit happen. Now that my family was gone, I didn't hit the beach as much, but I did seek ways to calm myself down because anything could set my PTSD issues off.

I remember when my family was still in Hawaii, I was going to make a point to have a very nice day with my family instead of just sitting on my La-Z-Boy chair. We headed to the beach down in Ko

Olina, and I decided to stop and put gas in my truck. Ever since I had been home from Iraq, I hated going to the gas station. If I could pay someone to take my car to get gas, I would. You have to understand, if you felt ten thousand pounds of explosives going off less than a quarter of a mile away, you would be scared of going to the gas station too. Well, again, I was in my hypervigilant mood, watching everyone getting gas. Cars came and went but somehow I my eyes were fixed on this truck approaching pump 10, and I was on pump 9. I noticed that the driver was smoking a cigarette and when he got out, he still had the cigarette in his mouth. He took out the gas nozzle in the back of his truck to pump fuel in a makeshift fuel tank. I asked him to please put the cigarette out. He stated that it was okay, he was pumping diesel fuel. I said, "Motherfucker, I'm pumping unleaded fuel." I was really about to put my hands on him and beat his ass, but I caught myself. I had my wife, daughter, and mother in-law in the truck with me and the best thing I could do at the time was to get in the truck, drive away, and get my family to safety. My plan was to put forty bucks in the truck, but I ended up put putting $17.10 in the truck, due to this asshole wanting to smoke a cigarette while pumping fuel.

This is why Soldiers like me with PTSD issues stay at home and cannot be bothered with the stupid and unsafe acts that people do every day. I did find ways to keep myself calm by heading to Ko Olina and hanging out on the beach in the evening, watching the sun set. I watched people enjoy their vacation in Hawaii and the ships go by in the ocean. When I saw the ships, I always wondered where they came from and how far they traveled.

While I was at the beach, I had my cell phone and I listened to some smooth jazz on Pandora. There would be times when I just sat there well after the sun went down. After experiencing a calm moment at the beach toward sunset, all I wanted in life was peace and quiet and to be able to laugh again instead of being mad at the world. I found out that it took up too much energy, and it was unhealthy to be mad at the world. It was bad enough that I saw more and more gray hairs at the age of forty-one. I used to be young looking before the Iraq War started—I was about thirty-one or thirty-two. Let's just say from age thirty-one to thirty-nine, my life was tied up being in Iraq, and from thirty-nine to forty-one, I had been fighting to get help for PTSD. That story will be in the next chapter.

I was home alone, struggling daily with my PTSD issues, and dealing with everyday life. I found myself needing help or daily assistance with everyday things. It almost seemed like I shouldn't be driving while having PTSD. It was hard to deal with traffic, and I didn't want any vehicles around me because it may be a threat. But if someone drove me around, it wouldn't bother me to get downtown.

I met a lady through a friend who had told her about me and the kitchen and bathroom remodeling that I did. We met up one evening and we just sat down and talked. I told her about my current kitchen job, about my PTSD issues, and my daily struggles. So she would call me on the weekends to see how I was doing. She asked what I was doing and I said that I was home, cleaning, doing laundry, and she said it was good I was staying busy. I didn't give it any thought, but later I found that hanging out with her as was good for me.

Prior to meeting her, I knew I didn't have any business being alone out in public because of the bad things that might happen, like putting my hands on someone for doing something stupid. If I was with someone, that person would intervene and have me walk away from the situation. Well, this new friend of mine would come from Kailua to my side of the island, Makakilo, and sit with me at Ko Olina and enjoy the sunset with me. We would sit and talk and laugh.

The following weekend, she took me to dinner at the really expensive restaurant in Ko Olina. It was really nice, and for the first time, being in public with tons of people around, I wasn't nervous on the edge or hypervigilant. Another weekend, we went downtown to Waikiki to walk around where all the nice shops are, looking at nice art pictures. It was something that I never was into, but it was nice to look at something that another person was interested in. Looking at art, I must say, really took my mind off my issues. After those three Saturdays went by, I caught on to what my friend was doing. It wasn't a date or anything like that. What she was doing was helping me to enjoy a weekend and to enjoy the moment like a night out on the town, having dinner, watching the sun set, or looking at art. I mean just having a weekend enjoying life. Most Soldiers who do multiple deployments to Iraq or Afghanistan don't know how to have a weekend, and if they do, it consists of binge drinking or partying like a rock star, messing with every drug on the street. To me, that has always been the wrong answer. There are also some who just stay home and look at TV. But when he is looking at the TV, he really isn't watching anything. His eyes are looking *at* the TV screen but his mind is in Iraq, and that's what happened to me when I was home. If I was not at home, I was on a side job doing a kitchen remodeling, bathroom remodeling, or anything to keep me busy to not have my PTSD issues catch up with me. There were times where I wished I was in Iraq putting in a fifteen-hour day and going to my room to sleep and then getting up and doing it all again. I liked that because I didn't have time to think other than about the next mission to come down.

I Lost My Cool with a Civilian While in Uniform

On 25 September 2012, I had to go upside a guy's head for calling me the N-word while he was riding his mountain bike down Makakilo Drive. I noticed that he was riding his bicycle in the middle of the road. The car ahead of him had gotten around him and when a third lane opened up, I got around him. As I was passing him, I said, "Sir, you need to ride your bike on the far-right side of the road."

He yelled out, "Fuck you!" called me an asshole, and gave me the middle finger. Now even though I was still calm and cool, being a professional Non-Commissioned Officer (NCO) in US Army uniform, the words and the middle finger that he gave me didn't bother me. But when I got down the hill, making a right turn by Chili's, the guy stopped and called me the N-word. I lost my cool. I'd be damned if I came home from four tours in Iraq with PTSD issues and let some guy say, "Fuck you," and use the N-word. I approached him and said, "All I needed you to do was ride your bicycle on the far-right side of the road."

He then took his helmet off and swung at me. I blocked it with my right hand and gave him a hard left to the jaw. When I did that I said, "Shit, let me stop." I had a witness and all I needed to see on the news was a black Soldier in uniform hitting a local guy. I just wished that people would learn to be respectful toward me and leave me alone to allow myself time to get my life back together in order to overcome this PTSD issue. The police got involved and no arrest was made, but I was so frustrated at how things were going with me. I would have been happy to get a free ride to jail. Maybe then I would have gotten some attention and been able to get some help with my issues.

The next day at five o'clock in the evening, I was coming off the freeway heading up the hill on Makakilo Drive and saw the same guy who had called me names the day before. He was riding his bike on the far-right side of the road, and I had to say, "Yes, street justice has been served." I guess that hard left to the jaw made him think twice about doing the right thing. That event made an impact on me, causing me to resolve that I would never get that upset with anyone again. When I was that upset, my head pounded with pain and I'd lose feeling in my right shoulder. My heart felt like it was going to pound out of my chest. I could have really blacked out and could have just killed him and walked away like nothing ever happened. The Iraq survival mode could really set in quickly when I felt a threat coming; all I wanted to do was kill. That was a bad feeling to have when I was out in public and all eyes were on me.

Wounded Warrior Transition Battalion (WTB)

WTB is known as a safe haven for all Wounded Warriors. In other words, if one gets wounded in Iraq or Afghanistan, then they would be qualified to go to WTB for proper treatment and healing. The location of the WTB at Schofield Barracks was heart-stopping. WTB's location was right across the street from Hamilton Field. Hamilton Field was the field where the 84th Engineer Battalion had PT formation every morning. While I was with the 84th Engineers (March 2004 to December 2010), I did three tours to Iraq with them and during the time just before PT formation, Squad leaders and other NCOs would be preaching, "You Soldiers better not go to them trailers to use the bathrooms." They were referring to the WTB. Soldiers would walk from their barracks along the side of the palm trees that lined up on the left side of Hamilton Field and pee right on the trees. So as you can see with the 84th Engineer Battalion, WTB was like a big hush-hush deal when it came to Soldiers who needed help from the WTB. 84th Engineers believed that leaders never showed any weakness, and the Battalion motto was: "Never daunted!" I've always stood by that motto and still do to this day, but a true leader should step forward and say, "Hey, I need some help." And the chain of command should support his or her needs. That was what I had been screaming for, for the past three years and someone outside the 84th Engineers finally listened to me. "Suck it up and drive on," just does not cut it after serving four tours in Iraq or Afghanistan.

On 26 September 2012, I finally started the process of getting treatment for other service-connected injuries, but mainly I was there for Post-Traumatic Stress Disorder (PTSD) at the Wounded Warrior Transition Battalion at Schofield Barracks in Hawaii. If you take a look at the timeline back in November 2009, when I came off my fourth tour in Iraq with the 84th Engineers of Schofield Barracks in Hawaii, I tried to get help way back then, but the chain of command at that time knew my end of service with the Army was December 2010, and they all said the US Department of Veterans Affairs (VA) would take care of me. In so many words, the military was going to boot me out without thinking about my mental health needs and let the next department handle the problems that occurred during my service for the military, or what some would say, "Pass the buck down to the next person to handle it." It took me three years to get into WTB, but I had to get out of active duty status and get into the Army Reserves.

After a year into the Reserves, LOD (Line of Duty) papers needed to get started so treatment could begin for PTSD. An LOD is for all Guards and Reserve members returning from mobilization and combat duty that encounter new challenges once they demobilized, especially if injuries or illnesses such as combat-related psychological health issues required further or additional medical care.

Now, I don't understand why an LOD would take over nine months to get done at the 9th MSC. I know it had a lot to do with the Two-Star General who could not seem to stay in her office long enough to sign the documents, so that orders could be cut for me to get into the WTB. In the nine months while I waited to get my LOD papers approved, there were many days I was at my unit and just wanting to throw someone off the second floor, due to their lazy asses sitting behind the desk, looking at a computer screen all damn day and creating excuses as to why they couldn't accomplish their jobs. This went for government status employees (GS) as well as some high-ranking Officers and Senior Non-Commission Officers. Well, you've read my story about the 9th TSG, BUT I WILL...talk more about the Two-Star General later.

On the second day at the WTB, all the wounded Soldiers had to attend a briefing. It gave me a chance to see all the Soldiers who were assigned to the WTB. In some of the Soldiers I could see the wounds, like some were using a walker or wheelchair. A few had prosthetic limbs, and it really showed me what the true cost of freedom was—something that the American people did not see on a daily basis.

Other wounds you don't see are the invisible wounds, knows as PTSD. Well, you can see the invisible, but you have to know what you're looking for, like the person's eyes—their eyes can tell you a lot. They constantly will be watching, especially if they are in a large group of people. They can't sit still, and if they were talking, you should listen to the words they are saying and how they are saying them. Most of all, they are quiet. When they are tense, their hypervigilance kicks in and they tend to breathe really shallowly. That was an everyday thing with Soldiers like me.

As the briefing began, the person conducting the briefing asked all the Soldiers what made them happy in the last twenty-four to forty-eight hours. There were over fifty Soldiers and they all said what they were happy for. But when it came to me, I said, "I've done four tours in Iraq. I've spent three years fighting to get help for my issues with PTSD, and I know I'm here in the WTB with an open mind for my treatment for PTSD." When the briefing was over, a female Soldier from Guam asked me if she could give me a big hug. It was a weird question, but I said, "What the hell?" She gave me a hug and I asked her what the hug was about. She said she heard what I said in the briefing about me waiting three years to get help with my issues with PTSD. She told me she had friends who came home from Afghanistan all messed up. They all had a hard time reintegrating with civilian life, so they started drinking heavily and doing drugs and allowing themselves to get in trouble with the law. Some lost their Army careers. Some committed suicide. She also said she was proud of me because I didn't go that route. I stayed in the fight to get help, and I never gave up. She told me I gave her hope and the motivation to stay positive and beat this thing called PTSD. I never thought I would see myself as a role model or a sign of hope. I really didn't see myself like that at all, but in some way I guess I was.

During the next two weeks at the WTB, as a Wounded Warrior, my job was to complete the in-processing stage in the WTB. My job consisted of setting up all my appointments and having an appointed nurse case manager who would manage my medical process. I was set up with one-on-one counseling as well as group counseling. I was also appointed a primary care doctor. In the WTB, that was how every Soldier was set up and that was how the WTB operated. Like every other operated program or system it's never perfect, but you do have your good days and bad days.

As the processing went on, somehow the Inspector General (IG) came to the WTB to find out if the Soldiers were getting fair medical treatment. Well, with me being new to the WTB, I never knew any problems that the Soldiers had in the WTB, though I did ask a very important question to the Inspector General. "Is the staff at the WTB out for the best interest of the Soldiers or are they out for the best interest of the Army to save a buck by downplaying Soldiers' illnesses and injuries?" The conference room got quiet, and the Inspector General didn't have too much to say. I also told them that once we had the answer to that question then other issues could be solved more smoothly and that could improve the Soldiers' medical treatment. During that time, my guard was way up like I didn't trust any staff members, like the nurse case managers or social workers and counselors. It was hard to figure out where their hearts and minds were for all the wounded Soldiers. In other words, whose side were they on?

I could see how the WTB was another safe haven for all the staff, like the GS employees and counselors, and the primary care doctors were contract employees. The WTB was a heavily funded organization, which meant the staff had a steady paycheck during each fiscal year. The reason why I say this is because I made an eye doctor's appointment about the eye problem that occurred on my second tour in Iraq (May 2004). I had two bumps on each eyeball, and I wondered if it had been getting worse over the years. The doctor looked at it and asked me a few questions, like how long I had been on this island. I told her since February 2004. Her evaluation was that I had been on the island too long, and Hawaii was constantly sunny. I was highly upset with her evaluation because she didn't ask the right question, like had I served in Iraq or Afghanistan.

And if so, how many tours? What people didn't see or understand was that in Iraq and Afghanistan, the heat from the sun was totally different than in Hawaii. I didn't know how to explain to an average person how luminous the sun was and what it felt like to be in 130- to 140-degree weather in full gear, doing construction. During my first and second tours, no one told us how important it was to wear our dark shades (sunglasses or eye-protection gear) during the daylight hours. No one ever told us to keep our shades on or that the sun would dry out our eyeballs. But during my third and fourth tours, I made sure my shades were on at all times. As you can see, that's what I mean by "downplaying our medical issues."

Come to find out, I was suffering from dry-eye syndrome, and I had to find that out from the VA when I did my head-to-toe physical. So again, that was another form of passing the buck down for the next person to take care of. So now the side effects of the dry-eye syndrome was that my eyes could not stand the sunshine and, at times, I saw beaming lights. My eyeballs were drying out and had developed cracks as if I had dry skin, but the dry eyes caused my eyes to be red as if I had been smoking weed all day. So now I had to insert eye drops in my eyes daily for the rest of my life.

During my thirty-day in-processing, I had a meeting with the chain of command and all the staff that were involved with my treatment plan for PTSD. The staff that would be working with me was a nurse case manager, social worker, primary care doctor, and medical board personnel. During the meeting, they all kept asking me what my goal for treatment was. I told them I wanted to overcome my issues stemming from PTSD, but they kept asking me the same question, so I asked them, "What are my options?" I asked that question because it felt like playing a game we were trying to win but didn't know the rules to. I found out later the purpose of that question, and what they were really asking, was after treatment if my plan was to return to duty or pick another job in Military Occupation Specialty (MOS) or take medical retirement. I thought about it really hard and looked at the health hazards that PTSD caused on one's body and saw how it affected my family and how it affected me just wearing the uniform while at Schofield Barracks and at my old Reserve unit.

I decided I would take a medical retirement. I figured, if a Soldier had seventeen years of service and four tours in Iraq, he or she has put in more work than a Soldier who spent twenty years in service with never one day in combat. And when I looked around Schofield and other duty stations, I saw high-ranking Officers or Senior Non-Commission Officers walking around with no combat patches on their right shoulders, and those were the ones who couldn't tell me shit about being a leader. Meanwhile, the war in Iraq and Afghanistan was still going on. I will talk about Non-Combat Soldiers and retirement benefits later. Once my treatment plan was established, the chain of command and the medical team supported my decision for medical retirement and began to focus on that direction. When I finally met up with my one-on-one counselor to make a final decision for my medical retirement, I gave the counselor my first twenty-five pages of my issues with PTSD, and I told her I wanted her to read it before my first appointment with her. I mentioned to her that most of the questions she would want to ask me were already in the twenty-five pages.

I did that because I had been around a few counselors and medical staff, and they seemed to ask twenty different questions, which irritated the hell out me. The twenty-five pages helped the counselor make a fair decision to have me retired and come up with a good treatment plan for PTSD. I had my first appointment with her, and she was surprised with the struggles I had with PTSD and how my old unit, 84th Engineers, didn't seek to get me help. I mentioned how I spent three years fighting to get help and, to top it off, I wrote a journal about my issues that helped the counselor a great deal with planning a streamlined treatment for PTSD.

Now, my twenty-five-page journal became a story book and writing about my problems and keeping a journal was the first step of the healing process, which meant I was ahead of the game, but I didn't know until later into the treatment process. I had other medical issues that tended to be undermined or downplayed on the

Army side. In other words, if I didn't speak of it, then they wouldn't say anything about it. But yet the medical problem was in my medical file to which they had access. It was almost like that old saying: "The squeaky wheel gets the grease." That meant if I spoke about my back and neck issues enough, then a treatment plan would be put in place. I guessed I was still on that good Soldiering shit ("Suck it up and drive on.") However, on the day-to-day stuff that went on at WTB, as a Soldier with PTSD, I just struggled trying to maintain and make it through the day at Schofield Barracks before things just got to me.

My spinal issues were worse than I thought after learning what they were and the treatment plan for them. The problems I had were arthritis in both knees, arthritis in my cervical spine, arthritis in my lumbar vertebrae, and tinnitus.

In November 2012, I was diagnosed with arthritis in my lumbar vertebrae. According to WebMD, arthritis like this is defined as "arthritis of the spine is a breakdown of the cartilage of the joints and discs in the neck and lower back" (WebMD, LLC, 2013). I researched possible treatments and discovered that many people recommended laser spine surgery. However, it was never offered to me while on active duty. I suffered many sleepless nights and headaches that would last for weeks due to my arthritis. I learned that arthritis in the cervical and lumbar spine could degenerate and lead to arthritis in the neck, which may also lead to osteoarthritis, including cervical spondylosis and degenerative joint disease. Another strange symptom I experienced was my pinky finger going numb for no reason. However, the research I did stated it might be "cervical bone spurs (osteophytes)." They are a common marker of cervical osteoarthritis, and cervical osteophytes may impinge on a nerve, producing the symptoms that radiate into the arms. Lastly, according to WebMD: "Arthritis in the lumbar and arthritis in the cervical spine normally affects people over the age of 45." I was age thirty-three when I did my first of four tours to Iraq, during which I conducted construction missions in full combat gear. By age forty-two, spinal injury was diagnosed but not treated. It made me feel frustrated to know that I did not receive proper care like a professional football or basketball player would.

Another illness I have that I have forgotten to mention is sleep apnea. Sleep apnea is a common disorder in which you have one or more pauses in breathing or shallow breaths while you sleep. Sleep apnea is usually a chronic condition that disrupts your sleep. When your breathing pauses or becomes shallow, you'll often move out of deep sleep and into light sleep. Breathing pauses can last from a few seconds to minutes. They may occur thirty times or more an hour (National Heart, Lung & Blood Institute, 2013). I had a sleep study done back in March 2010. My Battalion aid station from the 84th Engineers had to do the referral for me to do the sleep study at a local hospital in Honolulu. When the sleep study was complete, I figured the sleep study report would be forwarded to my Battalion aid station since they were the ones who did the referral. There was never a follow-up, so I spent another year or so dealing with disrupted breathing at night while sleeping.

Sleep apnea is hard on your body, especially your heart. It is hard to pump oxygenated blood throughout your body if you stop breathing numerous times through the night for thirty seconds or longer. In 2011, I had another sleep apnea test done through the VA, and this time I didn't know how to read the results, and the doctor didn't sit down and walk me through it. I ended up doing the footwork on getting the initial results from when I was an active-duty personnel so I could have the two results and hopefully someone would show me if my sleep apnea got worse after the second test from the VA.

When I met with my nurse case manager at the WTB, I gave her the sleep apnea results and when she reviewed it, the first thing she asked was if I ever got a breathing machine. I told her no and she was surprised I didn't get one from the VA. But I can tell you, thanks to my nurse case manager, I received the CPAP breathing machine a week later and started using the breathing machine the first night.

CPAP stands for "Continuous Positive Air Pressure." It is a gas mask-like device with a machine that pushes air into the nostrils to keep the airway open during sleep at night. The machine prevents obstructive sleep apnea (OSA), which is the result of blocked airflow during sleep, such as from narrowed airways. Other things, such as obesity, often contribute to obstructive sleep apnea. As a US Army Soldier, I'm far from being obese. I believe I have another form of sleep apnea that is called central sleep apnea, which results from a problem with how the brain signals the breathing muscles. This type of apnea can occur with conditions, such as heart failure, brain tumors, brain infections, and stroke (Mayo Foundation for Medical Education and Research, 2013). At the moment, I don't have a heart problem or brain tumor, and I never had a stoke other than Bell's Palsy, which is almost another form of a stroke. I believe that PTSD, along with nightmares, could trigger sleep apnea. When having a dream about an event that occurred in Iraq or Afghanistan, I would develop slight breathing trouble because in my dream I was trying to not be seen or heard, like hiding in the dark from the enemy or being involved in a heavy fire fight. All I wanted to do was shoot to kill, so a lot of stuff is going on in my dreams, and the last thing on my mind is breathing. With that said, I was holding my breath; it was a moment of natural respiratory pause while breathing, when most of the air had been exhaled from the lungs and before inhaling. So once again, that is why combat Soldiers are trained to breathe shallowly as well as how to be super quiet and not to be detected by noise since breathing makes noise. Have you ever seen scary movies and a person is running from something, and he hides in the dark but the bad guy manages to catch him because he is breathing too hard or too quickly? Well, that's why we breathe shallowly. Adults who have sleep apnea may snore loudly and have restless sleep with difficulty breathing. He or she may wake up with a headache or the person may be very tired throughout the day. I have experienced these side effects minus the fatigue in the morning. One of the real side effects I do have, when I don't use the CPAP, is that I feel pain in my left leg below the knee. My leg feels like I have been running all night, and it seems like I can't get my leg to function correctly until after ten in the morning—when I have been up since four.

I've learned that I've stopped breathing numerous times at night and my left leg was starving for oxygenated blood, which meant by me not breathing it caused my heart to work extra hard to pump whatever oxygenated blood was available. When you stop breathing for thirty seconds, that's a long time without oxygen in vital parts of your body like your brain and heart. My latest experience without the CPAP machine resulted in nightmares. My body tends to act according to what the dream is about, so my body and mind are in combat mode. Like I said before, when an event is about to take place, the last thing on your mind is breathing, so your muscle memory stops your breathing or it causes a longer pause in your breathing. When you're forced to wake up with a cough, your body will jump or violently jerk as if you're falling from a cliff in your dream. It wakes you up so you can start a normal breathing pattern.

The positive side of the CPAP machine is that when I wake up in the morning, I feel that good oxygenated blood flowing in my body, and my brain feels charged up and alert. I never have to think too hard about what I have to go do throughout the day. The five hours of sleep feels like twelve.

I believe I developed sleep apnea along with asthma after my visit to Camp Anaconda, Iraq, in 2004 and a second visit to Camp Anaconda in 2006. Both times, the burn pit had every conceivable type of waste piled high: plastics, batteries, appliances, medicine, dead animals, even human body parts were burned, with a dousing of jet fuel. A huge black cloud of smoke hung over the burn pit. It is funny how the Army is so strict on safety issues, yet the burn pit was able to operate without restrictions over the past few years without significant engineering controls being put in place like an incinerator (during my tour in 2004 and 2006). Seven years later, since my last visit in Camp Anaconda, I still have asthma right along with sleep apnea. But it took me three years to get the CPAP breathing machine, and now I still have that smoker's cough as if I have been smoking for years, but I have never smoked a cigarette in my life. The burn pit also causes allergy-like symptoms and breathing restrictions for which I have to buy over-the-counter medicine like Afrin. I have to have one in my truck along with my asthma medication on my bedside table.

I think the burn pit problem that causes pulmonary issues is like Agent Orange in Vietnam. It took years for our government to figure out that the health problems the Vietnam Vets had came from Agent Orange. By the time the government figured it out, most of the Vets had died from exposure to Agent Orange. Lawsuits have been filed against government contractors relating to the burn pits, but they were thrown out because as a government contractor working in combat zone, they were entitled to the same legal protection and immunity as US Armed Forces operating in combat. I wish the government could hold the Army's feet to the fire on the burn pit issues, and the government could help improve medical treatment regarding the burn pit and improve on compensation related to the health problems from the burn pits.

Tinnitus is the medical term for "hearing" noises in your ears when there is no outside source. Another name is "ringing in your ears." I was seeing a doctor who taught me to relax for thirty minutes when the ringing in the ears came around, but I found out on my own that the ringing did not have anything to do with the tinnitus in my left ear, or at least I think not. What I learned was that the ringing in my left ear has a lot to do with my PTSD, which causes my hypervigilance to kick in. My hearing turns up at a high volume along with my sense of smell—these are all the senses that kick in when you're in combat. They are the same senses that help you survive in combat. My first discovery of the ringing in the left ear was when I was at a crowded restaurant and I couldn't hear a word my wife was saying to me. When someone is talking to me, and if they are sitting on my left side, they will sound like Charlie Brown's school teacher. My hearing shuts off, and my left ear is ringing, but I hear conversations four tables down.

I remember when my wife and I visited my old high-school buddy in Omaha, Nebraska, and it just so happened that we visited during the weekend that Chris Tucker was doing a comedy show. The place was crowded and, again, I lost hearing in my left ear. My buddy was talking to me, but I didn't hear a word he said. However, I heard a conversation two rows up from where we were sitting. This guy told his buddy that he received a letter from the company he worked for informing him he was terminated from his employment. They didn't even fire this guy in person. I felt sad for him, but I felt extra sad because my hypervigilance kicked in, which caused me to look at everyone as a threat and listen to everything that was going on around me, waiting for something to happen so I could react to the threats. I've come to the conclusion that the things that trigger my PTSD and hypervigilance are things that I'm just going to have to live with. But the big problem is how to manage it.

My other physical injuries? Well, let's just say I can't do my job at combat speed like I used to, but I can do it at my own pace and take days off if I do so much work that my cervical spine starts to hurt. My other biggest problem is my hips, so if I'm having a bad week, then I'm down for a while. I don't think I will be having a job sitting at a desk, looking at a computer screen, and drinking Starbucks coffee. That's not me at all; I'm a Combat Engineer Soldier.

Everyday Grind at the WTB

I was assigned to ALFA Company and also assigned to an excellent Squad leader who made sure that all medical services and other treatments were available to me. I also met with the Company's First Sergeant. She was cool but at the same time I had a hard time putting my trust in her when she walked around with no combat patch on her right shoulder, while at the same time, we, as Wounded Warriors, who had been to Iraq or Afghanistan a few times were supposed to look at this First Sergeant as a leader. During that time, I never shared my issues from war with on Non-Commissioned Officers like her—who never spent one day in combat and had twenty years in service.

On the other hand, my Squad Leader had been to war a few times, so yes I put my trust in him and shared experiences that I had, and he could relate to some of the things I had been through. If I was having a bad day or was about to go off on someone, my Squad Leader would just say, "Hey, go to all of your appointments for the day and just go home." As time went on, Squad Leaders began to understand that coming into Schofield Barracks really put me on edge, meaning my "battle mind-set." I really didn't have patience with people, especially with the political drama that the WTB had to offer. Most of the time, if I was done with all my appointments by eleven, I would leave Schofield and head toward Ko Olina on the west end of the island and just hang out at the beach. Being at the beach was my grounding spot to get refocused and allow my anger and being on edge to calm down to where I could tolerate the stupidity and the drama that went on at Schofield Barracks. I don't know what it is, but there is something about being at the beach, looking at the ocean, that seems so peaceful. I would say because I'm from Oakland, California, I had always seen the ocean, but it is more than that. I believe it is therapeutic, peaceful, and calm. I guess that's what Soldiers like me need: a peaceful and calm environment, but that's hard to come by in this game of life.

First Day of PT Formation

The day prior, I was told where PT formation would be and what time PT formation was to start. The purpose of the first formation of the day was for all Squad Leaders to get accountability of all their Soldiers so that the Company Commander and First Sergeant would see that all Soldiers were counted for. I didn't bother to ask what the PT uniform would be because as a Soldier, you know what the uniform is every morning for PT. The first day of morning formation, I wore my black army PT shorts, my gray army PT shirt, my orange reflector PT belt, my white ankle socks that were Army Regulation-Standard, and running shoes. When I arrived at the tennis courts by Martinez Gym to meet first morning formation, I was at a loss. It seemed like I was the only Soldier in PT uniform. There were a few in the PT uniform but most were in civilian attire with regular gym shorts and T-shirts. It really opened my eyes to let me know that PT in the WTB was not the regular PT one would have in a regular unit, such as pushups, sit-ups, and at times, a four-mile run. Those activities didn't happen in the units at WTB because the Wounded Warriors had major injuries from war that prevented them from participating in those exercises. PT training for the Wounded Warriors consisted of seated volleyball, wheelchair basketball, and broom ball, but I think broom ball was mainly for the cadres at the WTB. There were also yoga sessions. I had never been to a yoga session. At times, I thought it was a waste of time, but I have heard from other people outside of the WTB that yoga was very good thing to be involved in. I guess I'm just not ready for that, but I can say it looks calm and peaceful and it seems that it helps you prepare for the daily madness.

During PT, I mainly did seated volleyball, but I noticed issues with my cartilage from my thigh bone to my hip bone and arthritis in my lower back. I can only play one game because the pain starts to set in, and then I'm pretty much not walking right half the day. Other days, we go to Wheeler Airfield for swimming and playing bocce ball. During those days, I would just go on a walk. It helped me calm down and get my thoughts together on what medical appointments I had that day and remember which questions I may have for each appointment. During the days of getting up and heading to Schofield Barracks and coming from the west end of the island, it was very dreadful the night prior, and it was hard for me to go to sleep at night because all my memories about Iraq kept replaying in my head, like one of my favorite songs stuck on replay. I believe that all my thoughts and issues with Iraq keep revisiting me in nightmares because most of our Construction Engineer missions were conducted during nighttime.

When I wake up in the morning, I'm enraged with a battle mind-set. If looks could kill, a lot of people would be dead before I even got to Schofield. With so much anger and rage I had in me every morning—due to fighting through traffic to get to Schofield on time—my mind would be so messed up that I couldn't function to figure out where formation was. I couldn't remember if formation was at the tennis court by Martinez Gym or if it was at Wheeler Airfield at the swimming pool. Not to mention, by the time I get to Schofield, I'm about to come unglued at the gate, and the only thing the person says to me is, "Welcome to Schofield." There have been times when I was so tense and enraged that I just wanted to vomit right at the gate. Sometimes I wish I would have vomited so maybe the side effects from war would have come right out of my system, and maybe I would be a much better person rather than wanting to cut someone's throat.

After our PT session, I would shower and get ready for daily medical appointments. I would wear my army combat uniform (ACU), and by wearing the ACU it put me in a war mind-set, wherein the inner rage and anger attempted to come out. I would forget that I was at Schofield Barracks and not Iraq. My medical appointments were close by Building 692, where other Wounded

Warriors received valuable information about their benefits for retirement and other services.

I parked my truck at one central location because at times I needed some information from Building 692 related to my retirement benefits. As I walked through the parking lot, trying to get to my appointments, my mind was not in the moment. My mind was thinking about which questions to ask about my medical issues. When I walked by an Officer, I'd forget to salute the Officer. The Officer would get bent out of shape and have a few words about me not saluting. I wanted to release my anger toward this Officer, but then I would be that guy in trouble and all it would do was make my day longer, and my day was long enough as it was, and it was only 8:45 in the morning. This problem happened two to three times a week for a period of two months, and all it did was add fuel to my fire—and someone was about to get burned.

On one particular day, I did lose control of myself in public while in uniform. I was in Kapolei to make my car payment at the bank. I always had a habit of parking my truck far away from other cars and buildings. It was something that I always did since my tours to Iraq. Also, I just didn't want anyone or anything messing with my truck. When I parked far away, I was constantly in hypervigilant mode, and even more so while in uniform.

When I walked into the bank, I visually scanned everyone from head to toe, looking for potential threats, as if someone was planning to rob the bank. I always had these thoughts in my head that one day I would be at a bank that was being robbed and everyone would be looking at me to save them because I was a Soldier in uniform. I would have saved the innocent people because I had raised my right hand, saying, "I, Jocephus Josey Duckworth, do solemnly swear that I will support and defend the Constitution of the United States against all enemies, foreign and domestic." When I left the bank, I constantly scanned the whole parking lot, looking at my truck to see if anything was wrong with it. When I got to the truck, I let my guard down too soon because some lady ran up behind me and said, "Excuse me, sir, but would you like to buy some cookies?" I went from zero to one hundred and had some nasty words for the lady. I mean, there are some things you just don't say to a civilian while in uniform. I told her she should not run up on a Soldier from behind since there were Soldiers coming home from war, and the last thing you want to do is run up on a Soldier from behind. In Iraq, the enemies had no uniform, which meant they were in plainclothes like everyday civilians, so after multiple tours to Iraq and being home from Iraq, I still treated "everyday Americans" as a threat. If I don't know you, you're a threat to me. It is something that develops in us as combat Vets that helps us stay alive during wartime. It is hard to turn that combat mode off when your home. The lady who ran up on me just thought I was a crazy Soldier from war, but I didn't care

Later, after I got home, I felt like shit. I was in uniform bad-mouthing a civilian. I almost swung and backedhanded her, and all she wanted to do was sell me some cookies. From that day forward, I chose not to wear my uniform in public, as well as at Schofield Barracks, while attending all my medical appointments. The next morning at PT formation, I came to PT in regular civilian attire. I had on black shorts, running shoes, and a beige T-shirt. I had worn the same outfit throughout the day, and every day it helped me be invisible, just like my wounds, while walking to my appointments. I did not have to salute any Officers as I walked by. Wearing my civilian attire during duty hours helped me stay calm and peaceful. My daily job while on active duty at the WTB was to attend to all my medical appointments, and if I was done with my early afternoon appointments, I would leave Schofield and not return until the next morning for PT formation.

Building 692

Building 692, known as the SFAC, was the main hub where all Wounded Warriors could come to get information on retirement benefits. The employees there helped Soldiers enroll in college courses, VA claims, and financial matters like VA home loans. You can also receive service from the chaplain if needed. Once a month, social security people would come out and help Soldiers file for social security benefits. The SFAC also has the Army Career and Alumni Program, which helps Soldiers with building resumes and posts updates about when the next job fair is. These were all resources that we, as Wounded Warriors, used to prepare for a smooth transition to the civilian workforce after leavening the WTB. But the true question was if the workforce was ready for retired Soldiers to hit the ground running, to show how skillful we were and the leadership experience we gained while serving our country. I will talk about the so-called potential job openings for fellow combat Vets in the civilian workforce later.

Worksite

Worksite is another resource or program available to all Wounded Warriors. It's mandatory for all Wounded Warriors to have a worksite when in between medical appointments. The worksite is also a working tool to help get your foot in the door for future employment on the government side of the house, and the only requirement for a Soldier is to put in a twenty-hour workweek. Soldiers can only have a worksite if it is a government-status business. For example, a Soldier can work somewhere in the FBI or work in logistics at Pearl Harbor or get his foot in the door for Homeland Security. If you're a computer geek, you can be in tech for any of those government organizations.

Having a worksite is a great program, but not for all Soldiers. If you look at the Wounded Warriors in the WTB, most of them are American Samoan Soldiers who were infantry men, so if they had gotten injured during combat and received medical treatment while waiting for their early retirement orders to come in, they would head back to American Samoa, which means they're not trying to ever work again. The key word is "retirement." When they go home to Samoa, they would be going back to their family's property that they've been raised on for many years, and that means they don't have mortgages to pay on their land or home. They can sit back and enjoy the retirement life, being with all their family members. It's the same situation for Guamanian and Saipan Soldiers.

The worksite program only benefits Soldiers like me, because after retirement, I have to work. The cost of living is high in some parts in the United States, but at the same time I'm not trying to work for another government agency. Working for the Army is a big headache by itself, and I don't need more work drama from the government.

My worksite was at Department of Public Workers (DPW) at Schofield Barracks. I worked in the air condition section with an A/C technician. He was pretty cool but other staff thought I got hired on. I noticed some of them gave me mean looks like, "How did he get this job?" or I heard conversations such as, "Hey, I thought the government did a hiring freeze." Some were unhappy because some were trying to get their family members hired on, but I came in out of the blue. They later found out that I was a Wounded Warrior from WTB, and after that, everyone started to be a little friendlier toward me. But it helped me understand more about why I couldn't get hired on back in 2010, because they spent more time hiring their buddies and family members. Never mind that I was a combat Vet and looking for work too. As time went on, I ran across a few DPW employers I worked with back in 2007 while working in the 9000 block, laying vinyl tiles in the living quarters. It was nice to talk with someone who knew me and how skillful I was.

I ran across an old Veteran who used to be with the 84th Engineers back in the 1990s. He said it wasn't hard at all when he got out of active duty and started working for DPW. I told him that it seemed like it took an act of Congress to get a job working for DPW, and I was getting the feeling that my fellow Soldiers who served in Iraq and Afghanistan were getting the short end of the stick when it came to getting jobs after military service.

When you compare it to the Veterans who served in Desert Storm, that war was over and government jobs were wide open for those Veterans, which explains why it is hard to find government jobs for Veterans who served in Iraq and Afghanistan.

I spent about two months at my worksite. I became less and less interested in the work because I knew there would not be a chance in hell I would ever be employed by DPW; there was a hiring freeze. The government shutdown caused government employees to go on required furloughs. Besides those reasons, the other reason was how the hiring systems worked. In other words, if a position opened, by law, they had to advertise it to the public on the Internet. So Soldiers like me, as well as others, would submit a resume and complete the application online and wait. While I waited for a few weeks, the HR department who oversaw the incoming resume and applications may have looked at my resume, but what they were truly looking for was their family member's resume. So that was why it was hard to get in where you fit because companies on this island had more relatives working for them than they do Vets. Remember, this was just my observation.

I was tired of the negativity I had about Veterans struggling to find work shortly after retirement. I had hoped to have at least a foot in the door to work for DPW, but I saw there was no future in working for DPW. I came up with an idea to do some mentoring at Job Corps in Hawaii, since I had been a former Job Corps student back in 1992 in Utah. I figured, instead of having so much negativity about no work for Veterans, I could choose to create positivity by mentoring young adults in Job Corps. Job Corps is a program administered by the United States Department of Labor that offers free-of-charge education and vocational training to youth, ages sixteen to twenty-four. Some Job Corps teach trades like carpentry, training to be an electrician, a plumber, an auto mechanic, culinary arts specialists, medical assistants, and many more.

One day I sneaked away from my worksite at Schofield to meet up with the center director of Job Corps. I gave the director a good history about myself and informed him that I also was a former Job Corps student. I also mentioned one of the things I wanted to do soon after my military service was to give back to Job Corps, mentoring and letting the students know that they can have a successful life and career after Job Corps. I believed that Job Corp truly helped me achieve a good jumpstart on life, and now I was soon to be retired. The center's director was extremely happy and was so blessed that I took time out to mentor some students, but she had a trick question for me. She asked me, "Who was the center director of the Clearfield job when you attended Job Corps as a student in 1992?"

I told her John Crosby but that I never set foot in his office because I never was a bad student. She said, "All right," and laughed.

I guessed that was a trick question to prove that I was a Job Corps student from back in the day. I was allowed to talk to fifteen students in the facility maintenance trade. The students learned skill trades like plumbing, electrical work, and carpentry all in one shop, which came in handy for me because of my background as a Construction Engineer in the Army. We could talk about construction all day long. I talked to the students in the facility maintenance trade, and they were fun to be with. I explained to them how I was a former Job Corps student from way back in the day. I talked about which trades I had completed, and they talked about me having a rough start trying to get a job after Job Corps. But I explained how I never gave up and the skills I had learned in Job Corps led me to greater things in life, like joining the Army and having the job I had at that moment. I talked to them about my military career, different places I'd been, what I had built, and about our time in Iraq as Construction Engineers. I also allowed them to watch my fifteen-minute video of some of my construction projects in the Army as well as side jobs throughout the years, like kitchen remodeling, bathroom remodeling, and other full-scale remodels. They liked the video and they all had a chance to see it firsthand that the Army had Construction Engineers, a fact that not too many Americans know about.

I took the students to my big, white Dodge truck that was loaded down with tools. When the students saw my truck with nice shiny rims and tinted windows they said, "Man, I want this truck," or, "Hey, I'm gonna get me one just like this."

I shook my head and told them, "Look, when you complete your trade and have a job, don't buy a big truck like mine." I explained to them that my truck cost big money every time it started up, around $126 to fill it up, the $377 truck payment, $1,500 for tune up, top-of-the-line brake shoes, new tires that cost $900, oil changes every 3,000 miles for $80. I opened up the lid cover so they could look at the tools that I had bought for myself throughout the years. I told them I had so many tools in the back of my truck that I could build a house.

I shared that this is what I gained from doing side jobs for years. I explained that they were in a perfect trade field and that the skills that they would learn would take them far, as long as they stayed focused and never gave up. During the three hours I spent with the students, I felt more alive than I ever had before. I didn't feel like the mean Staff Sergeant Duckworth from Iraq. I didn't even worry about all the drama at WTB or my issues with PTSD. I don't know how to explain it, but I felt free of all stress and worries when I was with the students. I guess somehow that was the only way I could put my problems aside and try my best to help others reach their goals or help solve their problems.

A month went by and I was able to return back to Job Corps to talk to eighty students. Now, I'm not a speaker per se, and I have talked to Soldiers throughout my military career, but it was a different type of talk with these students. During my lecture, I gave a brief history of myself, about being a Job Corps student, as well as an overview of my military career. I showed them the same video that the students saw in the maintenance facility trade, and a majority of the students liked it. I had some construction projects in the video from the Marshall Islands and there was a student from the Marshall Islands who recognized some of the projects that I had been involved in. After the video, the students understood that I had done construction projects all over the world and had done projects from one extreme to another, and all this after completing Job Corps in 1993.

After my lecture, I found out that out of eighty students, eight wanted to join the Army and do construction. My first thought was that I hadn't been trying to advertise the Army as a career choice; I just wanted to talk to the students and let them know that there would be a brighter life when the Job Corps program was completed. Yes, there would be some challenges, but if they stayed focused life would come with some rewards. Talking to the students at Job Corps was fun. I wish I could do mentoring for Job Corps students all over the United States. I believe that students need some type of hope, that they too can be successful in life after Job Corps training. I wished I could substitute teach in a carpentry trade or facility maintenance trade. It gave me some type of momentum and put some distance between my issues with PTSD and my everyday life.

Special Guest at the WTB

During January of 2013, we had three special guests. One was the Two-Star General from the 9th MSC. The General gave a speech to all the wounded Soldiers who were under her command, stating that she would foresee that all proper care and treatment was given to all her Soldiers, and if there were any problems to please let her know. I thought, *Yeah right, whatever. Look how long it took me to get into the WTB waiting for her final signature for orders for me to get in the WTB for my proper treatment.*

After her speech, Soldiers asked her if she could follow up on their Purple Heart awards from being wounded in a roadside bombing in Iraq. Now most of the Soldiers were American Samoan Soldiers stationed in American Samoa way down in the South Pacific, and I got the feeling that they were being forgotten even though they were wounded in Iraq. I have to say that shit didn't sit too well with me. I wondered how the chain of command was so slow on following suit on these Soldiers' Purple Heart awards.

The Purple Heart is awarded by the President of the United States to any member of an Armed Force or any civilian national of the United States while serving under competent authority in any capacity with one of the US Armed Services. After 5 April 1917, anyone who had been wounded or killed or who died or may hereafter die after being wounded should receive the award. The Soldiers had been waiting for over a year. A similar situation happened to a few Soldiers in Guam and Saipan. I was so mad that it felt like my blood was boiling. My heart was racing and I was so tense that my right shoulder went numb. I couldn't believe how these Soldiers were being mistreated with their Purple Heart awards.

Now, keep in mind these Soldiers were under the Two-Star General's command. This situation brought memories back from when one of my Soldiers was hit by shrapnel in a roadside bombing in Iraq 2008–2009. He was the Battalion Commander's Driver from 84th Engineers (Lieutenant Colonel). The Battalion Commander received his Purple Heart a few months before we left Iraq, and I remember seeing my Soldier around 2011 at the Army Tripler Medical Center in Honolulu. He had said that he received his Purple Heart Award two weeks before. I just want to say, it should have been a much faster process for our fellow Soldiers who had been shot or hit during roadside bombings or with rocket-propelled grenades to receive their Purple Heart.

After the speech from the Major General, I was able to have a few words with her. I asked her when the last time she had been to American Samoa was. She said she couldn't remember. Then I asked her if she knew who I was, and again she said she didn't, even though I was under her command. Her office was on the third floor and my office was on the second floor in Building 1557 at Shafter Flats. The Two-Star General also saw me working on the elevator, installing new tiles and brighter lights. I shook my head and said, "Ma'am, I'm Staff Sergeant Duckworth," and I told her that she had been in American Samoa in June 2011. "You flew in on a Thursday night and I was getting on the same plane heading back to Hawaii."

I asked the Major General if she noticed any new changes at the Reserves Unit in American Samoa, like new vinyl tiles in the conference room and the computer lab, as well as the classroom. She said she noticed them and they looked nice but she thought a contractor came in and did the work. I told her, "No, ma'am, it was eight Soldiers and me. We laid over 2,500 square feet of tile."

She had this dumb and confused look on her face. Like I mentioned earlier, Soldiers are not trained to lay floors; it just so happened that I, as a Soldier, had the skills and talent to lay floors and with other Soldiers like that under her command. She didn't take time out to know each and every Soldier's skill set and their capabilities, not to mention their situation in their military career, which clearly points to why these Soldiers under her command were still waiting on their Purple Heart awards. I was just so thankful that

I didn't have to serve under this Two-Star General in Iraq. I mean, this General was clueless about everything that was going on with her Soldiers, and I was glad that she had retired (thank God).

The following guest speaker was awesome. Her name was Congresswoman Tulsi Gabbard. She had served two tours to Iraq, and she truly understood the hardship that Soldiers went through in a time of war, as well as their injuries. Thanks to Congresswoman Tulsi Gabbard, she introduced and sponsored The Helping Heroes Act. It was designed to make it easier for wounded or disabled members of the military and Veterans to get through airport security screenings. At the time, I did not know how important the act was until I had to go through the airport security during the Christmas season of 2012. I believed that it did not make sense for Soldiers like me, and others with PTSD who served in the military and conducted multiple tours to Iraq or Afghanistan, to come home to the country they fought for and go through the same lines as regular civilians. There should be separate lines for active duty and retirees to go through airport security check and a less strenuous search.

When I went to the checkpoint, I had to stand in that round window for a complete body scan and when I came out, TSA personnel had to do a full-on body search as if I had something to hide. I asked him what the purpose of him doing a padded down body search was after I just came out of the rounded glass body scan? He said that it was normal procedure, and I told him it was a waste of money to have him on the payroll when the four million-dollar body scan was already in place to do his job. I also told him that he was doing a body search on a Soldier who fought for this country, which meant there were no signs of terrorist threats or actions in my DNA. I may have been a little harsh, but at that time I felt so disrespected. Furthermore, they ran my laptop computer through the scanner twice, as if I planted something in my laptop. My true question is: what type of line do all police officers, sheriffs, homeland security employees, and correctional facility employees go through for less of a body search?

The way I see it: all US Armed Forces retirees should go through that same line. Sometime after March 2013, when the Helping Heroes Act was in full effect, all airports nationwide along with the Transportation Security Administration (TSA) developed a plan to expedite screening to severely injured members of the US Armed Forces. In addition to offering curb-to-gate service for our nation's Wounded Warriors, these individuals would also be eligible to move through security checkpoints without having to remove shoes, light outerwear jackets, or hats. Well, I didn't get the curb-to-gate type service, but I had to say there was a drastic change at the security checkpoint for most of us travelers. I walked through the line without taking off my shoes and belt and didn't take anything out my bag. I guess having a retired military ID card that said "medical retirement status" had some privileges.

I believe that Congresswoman Tulsi Gabbard has been working hard in Washington to help preserve our military benefits as well as improve our retirement benefits. During her speech, she did mention that she would still continue to fight to protect our benefits while she was still in Washington. After the speech, a lot of questions were asked about Soldiers' Purple Heart and how it can be a smoother process to receive their Purple Heart. I wish I were on her staff because there needed to be better benefits when one was a Purple Heart Soldier. What I mean is, if I had it my way, Purple Heart Soldiers would never ever pay taxes, no state taxes, no property tax, no federal tax, and no sales tax. Furthermore, the interest on his/her home loan needed to be zero. American people need to understand these Soldiers took a bullet for their freedom, when an average everyday American didn't raise his right hand to be sworn in and say, "I will support and defend the Constitution of the United States against all enemies, foreign and domestic." I want the best for our Soldiers and have them highly recognized for their sacrifice and hard work.

After her speech, I was able to shake hands and have a few words with her. I gave her a small history of myself, told her about my tours in Iraq and my unit, and she asked me if my name was Joe. I asked her, "How did you know?"

She said that her dad was a senator from Hawaii who knew me. I was kind of shy and said, "Yes, I know your dad. I've sat in on his speeches from time to time." I also mentioned that I was writing a book about my struggles with PTSD, and I had to explain to her that that was the reason why I was in the Wounded Warrior Program. She said that she wanted to have a copy when I finished. I told her that when I was done with the book, I hoped to meet with Congresswoman Tammy Duckworth, another combat Vet. I wanted to meet her because we have the same last name; I caught hell when her Black Hawk went down in Iraq in 2003. Every Soldier thought she was my wife or sister or cousin. Congresswoman Tulsi Gabbard mentioned that she could arrange something like that. I think it would be nice to have picture of the two congresswomen on my wall, right along with my awards and other Army career items.

A few months later, Congresswoman Gabbard gave a speech at a breakfast banquet at the Hilton in Waikiki. All the top brass officials in the military were there, along with her dad. In her speech, she mentioned that she wished there were more war Veterans from Iraq and Afghanistan working in Washington. She said we needed fresh blood in Congress to help improve our retirement benefits, as well as our military benefits. I always wondered what it would be like to work on staff for a congressman or woman. If I had my choice, I would like to work on improving the Soldiers' retirement benefits and medical treatments. I think football players and basketball players receive better medical treatment and benefits than Soldiers, and all they do is play ball.

A few months later, we had a special guest at the WTB. He's known as Lieutenant Dan from *Forrest Gump*, an actor whose real name is Gary Sinise. Lt. Dan is one of the few actors I know of who is a big supporter of all the members in the Armed Forces. It was a Saturday. He and his band crew flew from Chicago to Hawaii to perform at Schofield Barracks. All the wounded Soldiers waited patiently at the library when "Lieutenant Dan" arrived from the airport, and we all gave him a warm welcome. When he came in, the first thing he said was, "Sorry I'm late, but I had to go pee." We all laughed because I think all of us remembered the scene when Forrest Gump said the same thing at the White House. Gary Sinise gave a nice speech on how he was a big supporter of us troops, and he also took time to take pictures. When it was time for my picture to be taken with him, I asked him, "Can I call you Lieutenant Dan?"

He said, "Sure." He laughed.

I told him, "I bet when you did *Forrest Gump*, you never thought you would be this famous."

He laughed and said that he had been really blessed with the character of Lieutenant Dan. Later that night, his band played at Martinez Gym. To sit there and watch him and his band play for all the Soldiers at Schofield Barracks was awesome. You could tell that man had tons of energy to fly from Chicago to Hawaii nonstop, only to spend four hours taking pictures with Soldiers and signing autographs. This man is a big supporter of our fellow troops.

Help Has Finally Arrived

Hallelujah, help had finally arrived for Soldiers with PTSD. Group sessions for PTSD started in October 2012. Keep in mind: I had been waiting three years to get any treatment for PTSD from the United States Army. My group session was twice a week for almost nine months, and each week I learned a lot about PTSD and other issues that came with it, along with why we as combat Vets still carried that inner rage from war. It was the same rage that kept us alive in combat but could lead us into trouble with the law if someone tried to aggravate us—which would lead to attack mode, or what I like to call, "the battle mind-set."

Our group session was a safe haven for all Soldiers with PTSD. We all could relate to one another about our struggles with PTSD. One infantry Soldier explained how the combat mind-set, or that inner rage, was so dangerous to have when you were put back into regular life and you still had that urge to kill. He said that it was just like allowing tigers and lions from the zoo to walk the streets in a civilian-populated area, just waiting for something to trigger them to attack. Talk about bloodshed on the streets!

The young Soldier said that having the combat mind-set and the inner rage, not to mention the adrenaline rush, all combined into the perfect storm. That combination was a good thing to have in the middle of a firefight. He said that in Afghanistan, a firefight could last from three minutes to three hours to three days or more, and during that time the "perfect storm" he had was what kept him alive in combat, but it was hard to shut it off. This was why, at times, I felt like I was a danger to society. With the four tours to Iraq and that perfect storm still swirling around me, I saw myself as that lion or that tiger walking the streets, waiting to go after someone because he or she looked at me wrongly. Like I said before, it was hard to shut it off after coming home from war.

Thanks to his sharing, it let me know that we have a lot of work to do to learn how to control the invisible wounds from war. What I had learned about our perfect storm prior to coming to group session was that when I did my four tours, I was a perfect Soldier in time of war. I did everything right; I functioned very well regardless of what event happened. I believed I functioned like a true combat Soldier, but each time I came home I was different, different because I couldn't shut the combat mode off—I couldn't shut the perfect storm off.

So six years later, when my fourth tour ended, everything that I experienced in Iraq just started crashing down so fast that if I acted on my emotions—anger and rage—I'd be put in jail for a long time. In group session, we learned what Post-Traumatic Stress Disorder was all about. PTSD symptoms typically start within a few months of a traumatic event(s). In a small number of cases, though, PTSD symptoms may not appear until years after the event. PTSD symptoms are generally grouped into four types: intrusive memories, avoidance, numbing, increased anxiety or emotional arousal (hyperarousal).

Symptoms of intrusive memories may include:

- Flashbacks or reliving the traumatic event for minutes or even days at a time
- Upsetting dreams about the traumatic event

Symptoms of avoidance and emotional numbing may include:

- Trying to avoid thinking or talking about the traumatic event
- Feeling emotionally numb
- Avoiding activities you once enjoyed
- Hopelessness about the future
- Memory problems
- Trouble concentrating

- Difficulty maintaining close relationships

Symptoms of anxiety and increased emotional arousal may include:

- Irritability or anger
- Overwhelming guilt or shame
- Self-destructive behavior, such as drinking too much
- Trouble sleeping
- Being easily startled or frightened
- Hearing or seeing things that aren't there

Post-Traumatic Stress Disorder symptoms can come and go. You may have more PTSD symptoms when things are stressful in general, or when you run into reminders of what you went through. You may hear a car backfire and relive combat experiences, for instance. My reminders are fireworks from Fourth of July or New Year's Eve. There are times where I have locked myself in my room, worn ear plugs, had the air conditioning on full blast, and watched television, just so I would not hear all the fireworks going off as if mortar rounds have hit multiple times. There have been times when these fireworks were so loud that I dialed 911 to explain that I was a Soldier with PTSD and I was doing everything in my power to not leave the house and walk down the street to cut someone's throat because they were firing off fireworks and did not have any respect for Soldiers who were home from Iraq and Afghanistan.

The police never came out but I tell you: if I had left the house and cut someone's throat, I know there would be four or five cop cars in the neighborhood, looking to kill me for what I did. I have to say, having those thoughts of cutting someone's throat and leaving them there to die is a very sick thought. If I acted on my sickly thoughts of killing, it would be more than just one person being killed because that combat mind-set kicks in as if I am still in Iraq—that "killer rage" and that adrenaline rush all working together. The sad thing about having those two deadly combinations is that nothing matters;

it doesn't matter that you have taken someone's life or you're going to jail for a long time. All you want to do is kill and when it's all done, you will go home like nothing ever happened.

A Soldier walking the streets with that type of mind-set and acting on his feelings and thoughts is like waiting for that perfect storm to erupt. I've learned that with my anger and rage issues, it seems like I would need a personal assistant to be with me out in public to be the middle man to help me solve my tax problems, home mortgage issues, or child support. Because if I did it myself, with PTSD, and with the battle mind-set, some nasty words would be said, which would cause me to put my hands on the person and I would be the one going to jail.

In my opinion, the easiest way I deal with money issues or government issues is I take care of the problem, but I send them a letter telling them I fought for this country and to please leave me the fuck alone. The bottom line is that I do need a personal assistant who can help me out on day-to-day stuff. A Soldier with PTSD doesn't think straight or clearly well enough, at least I know I'm not thinking clearly.

Another reminder is seeing someone walking on the overpass on the freeway; it truly bothers me when I see someone walking up there and they stop and look at cars as they drive underneath. The reason this bothers me so much is because back in Iraq in 2004 and 2005, there were many cases where the insurgents would see a convoy approaching the overpass and they would try to time it and drop a grenade in the turret where the gunners stood, and the grenade would explode and kill everyone in the vehicle. There have been incidents where the insurgents would run a thin cable wire across the road by the overpass just high enough to where it could cut the gunner's head off. So yeah, I can't stand to see anyone on the overpass, especially if they stop walking and look at traffic go by.

The worst reminder is seeing someone on the corner or walking and talking on the cell phone. Insurgents would use cell phones to call another cell phone that was attached to an improvised explosive device (IED) and blow the roads up, mostly aimed at convoys that were going by. Shit like that happened all day, every day in Iraq, and at times, I just wanted to shoot anyone with a cell phone. So just imagine me with an M16 or M4 here in the United States just shooting at someone for talking on the cell phone. The funny thing is, the people I truly want to go after are the dumbass people who like to pump gas and talk on their cell phones when there's a big sign by the gas pump that says, "No cell phone use at the fuel pumps." So this is why I need a daily personal assistant, just so they can pull me away from the problem or talk me out of it, because if I can act on my thoughts and feelings and get away with it, there would be a lot of dead bodies with my name on them.

Learning to Control My Anger

In learning about our struggles with PTSD, I realized that PTSD was like an onion; I would need to peel each layer of the onion to learn to resolve and manage each emotional issue until I got to the core. With four tours to Iraq, I knew I had a lot of work to do.

Destructive Anger

Destructive anger can blind you. It causes a disadvantage for you to get perspective or improve the situation. Once you're in control of anger, you can put it to positive use. In others words, before you have the feeling or the impulse to act on anger to hurt someone, your first priority is to regain safety of your anger in order to smooth out the situation. One example I can give you was when I was getting my taxes done for 2011 and 2012. The lady on the phone was talking to her relatives about what their plans were for the night at the same time she was working on my taxes, which meant she was not paying attention, in my opinion. I was afraid that she would get the numbers messed up and cause me to pay more. My first thought was to knock the cell phone out her hand, knock the taste out her mouth, and tell her, "Look, you are here to work and not socialize over the phone." But if I did that I would be that guy going to jail. But it's okay in this laid-back work ethics world we live in for this tax person to be on the company's time doing my taxes and talking on the phone. When she finally finished with the conversation, I was so mad my chest felt like it was on fire and my skin felt like it was burning. I hurried up and paid the lady and left.

Two months went by and I received a letter from the State Tax Commission of Hawaii. I called them asking them why I owed two grand in state taxes. My first thought was that dumb bitch fucked up my tax paper. Since I was on the phone with the state tax people, I told them they needed to stop shining the seat with their asses, do their fucking jobs, and do the numbers again. If I had to go up there to speak to one of them, it was not going to be nice. In fact, I would be walking out of the state building in handcuffs. After the conversation, I hung up the phone very pissed off. It seemed like every government agency was after every Soldier who served in Iraq and Afghanistan, and it seemed like they tried their best to get a rise out of a Soldier and watch him go to jail, knowing that most of us were diagnosed with PTSD.

Another month went by and I received a tax return check from the state. I was so happy because I knew my intuition was correct about them getting the numbers wrong. That is why I can't stand people having jobs where they sit on their asses and look at computer screens. They will be so quick to inform you that you owe money to the state. What they need to do is their jobs right the first time, before they call about money owed to the state.

So what I learned about situations like this was I would never go to a place where I knew my anger would get me in trouble. What I would normally do was e-mail or write a letter about the problem or issue. That way, if some nasty words were in the letter, the reader could be hurt by the words or would just throw the letter in the garbage. The bottom line, I would not be walking out of a building in handcuffs, heading to jail because I acted on my anger. Another method I used was if I owed something like back child support, I would send them a cashier's check, paid in full, and send a note saying, "Here's your money, now leave me the fuck alone."

Times When Problems Are Frustrating to Solve

When multiple problems do occur, it is not a simple fix or an on-the-spot correction. Your feelings like rage and anger want to boil over, and your emotions get the best of you. I learned doing activities that help you feel in control help to counteract the out-of-control feelings of destructive anger. A few things that may help ease the anger could be: cleaning the house, doing yard work, and writing a list of things to do. Doing these constructive activities helps to channel the negative energy to something positive, and when that occurs, you come up with a positive solution to some or all of your problems.

I remember one day I was so mad that I wanted to vomit, and somehow I just snapped and started washing my truck by hand. That truck was too big to be washed by hand, but three hours later after removing hard water spots, I was done. Since wearing my uniform stirred up many issues with PTSD, I decided that I wasn't going to wear my uniform while going to my appointments at Schofield Barracks. When I was done with all my appointments, I left Schofield Barracks and did not return until the next morning's formation.

Method of Time-Out

According to our counselors, having a time-out is one of the most effective strategies. Whatever happens, at all costs, you must delay any anger expression or action until you are back in the safe zone to handle the situation. We learned that it takes twenty to thirty minutes for the body to return to normal, but I thought time-out was kids' play. In the past, when my PTSD and anger issues kicked up, it took at least twenty-four hours for me to calm down. This explained that when I was with the 9th TSG, I would leave for the rest of the day, keeping me from putting my hands on people when they made things harder than it should have been to get things done.

At times, I would leave at ten in the morning and not come back until the next day. When things got really bad from being out in public and seeing stupid shit happen, I found myself locked up in the house for three or four days, not even leaving to get the mail. It's one of those things where if one person approached me and asked me a question or try to get me to buy something from them, I might just snap and go off on that person. So that is why when things get bad I just keep myself in the house. I guess you could say that I was protecting the civilians from myself. Like I said before, I feel like I'm a danger to society at times.

Express Your Anger Calmly

Expressing my anger calmly takes some serious work and extreme concentration. I spend most of my time watching my anger meter raise, monitoring my heart, and hoping it's not beating one hundred beats a minute. This explains the time-out method, regardless of how angry I am. My twenty-four-hour time-out gives me plenty of time to calm down and start the thinking process on how to work the problem out calmly with no anger involved. Most times, I take a time-out to explain what issues I have with a person without using any nasty words. Others times, I will talk face-to-face, but calmly and slowly so they can clearly understand what I say and understand where I'm coming from. But keep in mind that my heart is racing, my left ear is ringing, and my blood is boiling because my skin feels like it's on fire. I also understand that when I'm angry and yelling, people don't hear me; they only hear the yelling and nothing gets solved.

Grounding Techniques Help Detach From Emotional Pain

What is grounding?

Grounding is a multiple set of strategies to separate from emotional pain. Distraction works by focusing outward rather than inward toward you. This helps me understand what I was doing when things got so bad with my PTSD. I would still find an ounce of positive energy and help others when they called for my help; I would help them with anything.

By doing this, it caused a distraction from my issues and, at times, I found answers to my issues by helping others. Helping others has always given me a sense of purpose, regardless of how dark my life has been. When my services were helpful to others, it gave me a sense of accomplishment and self-worth.

Another method of grounding is healthy detachment. Prior to me knowing what healthy detachment was, I did special projects for a Sergeant Major in G3 section at 8th Theater Support Command at Fort Shafter back in 2009 and 2010, when I returned from my fourth tour in Iraq. I guess back then I needed that healthy detachment because I wasn't a good NCO at Schofield Barracks. I mean, there were times that I didn't choose the right words toward the lower enlisted Soldiers when it came down to chewing their asses out for being late to formation. It almost came down to putting my hands on Soldiers and losing respect of young Officers "Lieutenants," especially them "Butter Bars." I just did not have time for kids. Yes, I said kids. When I was thirty-nine years old and got a young "Butter Bar" age twenty-three or twenty-four, I just did not have time to hold them by the hand. There's a reason why in our running cadence (Battalion run), we would say, "You can't spell lost without the LT," referring to the Second Lieutenants who were very wet behind the ears since coming from West Point and other colleges.

Why Do Grounding?

The purpose of grounding is mainly for when you're overwhelmed with emotional pain. Grounding is a way to detach from emotional pain so you can gain control over your feelings and regain safety. Grounding methods will not work if alcohol or drugs are involved. Grounding is structured to help you be in the present and be conscious of reality.

An Activity that Helps Me with Grounding

I believe that every grounding activity and method is different from one PTSD Soldier to another. Grounding comes into play when something triggers me that puts me in that Iraq mode. I have to use the grounding method to put a healthy distance between those negative feelings and myself. What I've done to accomplish that is sit at the beach at Ko Olina on the west end of Honolulu. There's something about the ocean that makes me think that everything will be okay. Sitting by the beach and looking at the ocean truly keeps me in the moment. The ocean helps me regain that joy and happiness. I remember times when I left Schofield Barracks, enraged and with my head hurting, and after thirty minutes of being at the beach, I was laughing and joking with myself. There have been times when I felt so free at the beach that I stayed there well after sundown and never checked my phone for text messages or calls. Basically, I didn't want anything disrupting a good moment like that.

How Scuba Diving Became Part of My Grounding Tool

Before I learned about scuba diving, there was an infantry Soldier who served in Afghanistan. As we learned about the grounding technique, the Soldier explained how scuba diving was such a good grounding tool that he spent most of his weekends underwater at the North Shore in Honolulu. He gave such great details on what type of fish he saw underwater, as well as different types of organisms that lived around the coral reefs. At one point, I thought he was training to become a marine biologist, but then again when one is in a peaceful environment, everything looks bigger, brighter, and more interesting. As he explained his underwater adventure, he had no facial expression, but I could see the tense look in his eye, the type of look that every combat Soldier has after serving multiple tours in Iraq and Afghanistan. He had a plain monotoned voice like the teacher from *Ferris Bueller's Day Off.* "Bueller, Bueller, Bueller." After his stories, I made a point to take scuba diving lessons to become a certified diver, hoping it would take away some of my issues from war.

Thanks to the WTB, who financed the diving lessons for Soldiers who were interested in diving, I took the opportunity and signed up for diving lessons. I was issued a textbook and workbook, thinking that the first day of class was a classroom environment, so I spent Friday through Sunday getting the workbook completed before Monday evening. Monday evening came and we were all shuttled to a swimming pool in Kaneohe. I was really thrown off track because I had completed the nine chapters in the textbook for diving.

Our first training was around the swimming pool, getting hands-on training. The first day of diving training put me in military training mood. I think because it was a natural reaction. I needed to pay attention to detail because in sixty feet of water, the simplest problem could turn into a life or death scenario if the problem is not fixed ASAP. As the hands-on training continued, we learned the importance of each piece of equipment, like the buoyancy control device (BCD)—an expandable bladder that is inflated or deflated to regulate buoyancy. Another important thing we learned about diving was when dealing with the tank valve. The first thing one needs to look at is the O-ring. If there is no O-ring, there is no diving.

After the hands-on training with the diving equipment, the biggest training was to swim four laps in a pool that is half the size of an Olympic pool. I wasn't sure if these laps were time tested, so I gave it my all in speed and strength. On my third lap, I was so exhausted that my whole body shook like a wet dog on a cold winter night. I had been tired before, but nothing like that. On my third tour in Iraq, I did physical training, but I ended up heading to the aid station where they hooked me up to IVs, because they figured I was dehydrated. It took four bags of IV to get me stabilized.

After my third lap in the pool, I just couldn't do it. I was so weak it took me forty-five minutes to get my wet suit off. I told the instructor that I couldn't do it. I ended up dropping out of scuba diving class. I felt so embarrassed as a Soldier. I had never failed at anything related to training. I really started to ask myself, *Am I really that out of shape?* I was so messed up and so weak that if I knew the swimming pool street address, I would have called the ambulance to take me to Tripler Hospital. So as a Soldier I had to suck it up and wait until the training was over. The training was over around ten o'clock. We were there for four hours, but there was a forty-minute shuttle ride back to Schofield Barracks.

Once we arrived at Schofield Barracks, I was still feeling messed up when the bus driver dropped us off. He saw that I was walking so slow and hunched over, and he asked me if I needed a ride to my truck. I said, "Yes please, and thank you." I don't know how I drove home to Makakilo, but I just knew I was extremely weak and had cottonmouth. I wanted water when I got home but ran out of bottled water, so all I did was take a cold shower, hoping I would feel better.

I felt a little bit better after a cold shower. I turned on the air conditioner and slept naked in my bed. The coldness was the only thing working for me.

The next morning, I got up as normal, but moved twice as slow. I still felt weak from the night before, so I went to see my primary care doctor after calling in sick. When I saw my primary care doctor, I explained what had happened at the scuba training. The doctor told me that I just may have overloaded myself with activities. It's an everyday struggle to deal with things like appointments at the WTB and group sessions while keeping track of my retirement. There it was ten o'clock at night and I was still at the pool when my day had started at five in the morning. The doctor may have been right, but he should have given me four bags of IV to replenish my fluids and electrolytes. The only thing he gave me was a written note for me to have three days of rest. I felt like it was another way of doctors downplaying my illness by just giving me three days off. He should have replenished the fluids I lost when I overworked myself swimming laps.

After my three days of quarters (rest) at home, I came back to the WTB. The Soldiers with whom I was in scuba diving training were all asking me what happened because they said I looked so sick, and that night my eyes were blood shot. I told them I didn't know and I wasn't sick; I had just overdone it on the swim laps.

As weeks went on, I felt like a failure that I had not completed the diving course. I kept thinking, *Is this what has become of me? I'm a failure now?* I guess as a Soldier, I spent years of achieving high standards because that was what the United States Army expected out of me. One of the things I learned about failing the scuba diving course was how fast I could bounce back on top.

Four months went by. I wasn't going to allow the failure of scuba diving to get the best of me. I went to a diving place on the North Shore to find out when their next diving course was. The diving store was recommended by one of the nurse case managers at WTB. I would like to thank her very much for recommending the diving place on the North Shore. The diving class was a three-day event, and this time I had to pay the $275 for the course, so yes, I had to pass this course.

The first two days were so cool and so relaxing, but it was serious training in thirty feet of ocean water. The third day was awesome and most of our final training was underwater. The grand finale of our training wasn't swimming two miles in the ocean; it was learning how to stay afloat for ten minutes without any scuba gear. My anxiety kicked in when I found out about floating in the ocean for ten minutes. We all know most black men sink like rocks. We have too much muscle mass and the last time I checked, muscle weighed more than fat.

I told the diving instructor that I did not know how to stay afloat, and I shouldn't be out in the ocean trying to float and risk two instructors' lives who weighed a hundred pounds less than I did. I was really scared because I knew we had to swim two hundred yards out in order to do the final test and, not to mention, my $275 was on the line. I had no desire to fail again! I asked the instructor what the special trick was to stay afloat. He kept telling me to just get out there and relax. I could not comprehend the word *relax*.

When our lunch ended, we began heading down toward the beach. I was still racking my brain, trying to figure out how I could float and not put others in danger trying to save me if things went wrong in fifty feet of water. We swam two hundred yards to start our floating test. My anxiety was still high, and I asked the instructor again how I could stay afloat for ten minutes. Now, it's funny how someone can say the simplest thing that is as clear as a bell. What he told me was fifty feet underwater and two hundred yards out in the ocean, our lungs are like floating devices, "So float on your back, take a deep breath, breathe shallow, and relax."

When I got the vision of that, everything became clear to me. I floated for the required ten minutes effortlessly and peacefully. My mind was elsewhere, thinking about happy places like taking road trips and visiting a few of my Soldiers with whom I've served. When our ten-minute floating deal was over, I swam back to shore and felt a huge accomplishment—so huge, it felt like I had won the war. The next day, I went scuba diving. With all the pressure off of me, I finally got to feel what the Soldier in our group session was talking about being underwater. I felt calm and peaceful and not once did I think about events in Iraq or my struggles with PTSD. I was truly in the moment, focusing on everything underwater. I even saw a four-foot white tip shark, but sharks that small are more scared of us than we are of them. I even explored the life around the coral reef.

As you can see, I went through a huge ordeal to get the feel of what the Soldier was telling us about in our group session, and all we want is the feeling of being free and able to enjoy the moments of calmness and peace. Now it's funny how we have to discover a moment of peace and calmness in deep waters. Thanks to the Soldier, I've incorporated scuba diving into my life. I just need to get my money together to buy scuba gear. Right now, all I can do it rent the equipment out.

Another skill that I added in my grounding techniques was listening to smooth jazz. Thank God for Pandora. I normally leave Sundays for "smooth jazz Sundays," and I make sure I listen to Sade. When I do kitchen and bathroom remodeling, I always listen to Sade. Her songs help slow my mind down and not have it running at a hundred miles per hour. I also find her songs so soothing during stressful times throughout the projects. I find myself solving problems without an ounce of stress. Sade's music makes me feel like I can move mountains even after a hard day's work. Among other songs I find myself listening to are old school artists like AL B. Sure! and Keith Sweat. I try to listen to them on Fridays, and I call it "old school jams Friday." Their songs help me reset my mind back to my high-school days. I would rather think about those days than events in Iraq that keep replaying in my head, like a CD stuck on replay.

Group Outings

Group outings that were part of our PTSD program were on Tuesday and Thursday and our field trips were Monday, Wednesday, and Friday. The counselors kept getting upset with me because I continued to call them "field trips" as if we were back in grade school. The purpose of our field trips was for us Soldiers with PTSD to get used to being out in public. Going out in public was a good method, seeing that we were often hypervigilant and always scanning everything. When in downtown Honolulu, there was a lot to scan. Most of us didn't like it at all. Scanning things at downtown Honolulu was like scanning downtown Baghdad or downtown Mosul. What we were looking for were potential threats; we still look and treat civilians as threats. There have been a few times where we went to the beach in Waikiki but found ourselves scanning the beach when some kid or a group of kids were screaming because they were playing in water. We all focused on the scream, as if the kids were in danger. As a few of these group outings went on, it was hard for us to let our guards down and enjoy the moment of just being outdoors.

Manoa Valley

Manoa Valley was the first peaceful and quiet field trip we went on. We visited the home that conducted grand tours to the public. We entered the house, heading toward the backyard. As we sat in the backyard, it was nothing but pure peacefulness on a nice warm and sunny day looking toward the green landscaping. The mountain valley has a rare natural beauty that is hard to explain. Later, we had to go through the tour of the huge backyard that was well kept. The purpose of the tour was to learn the history of Manoa Valley as well as the house itself.

I didn't want to go on the tour because I really wanted to stay in the moment of peacefulness and quietness, because for the first time in a while, I could hear myself think. There was always someone who didn't recognize the peacefulness as they walked into a room of people, being in the moment of quietness, or an outside area that had a quiet moment. In my case, my moment of peace was disrupted due to me having to join the group and go through with the tour.

As I went halfway through the tour, I noticed a nice metal wooden bench under a tall tree that provided nice shade from the sun. I sat there as the tour went on to regain my peaceful moment. It lasted for about forty minutes until a landscaper worker started up his motorized weed eater that made a bunch of noise. By then, I said to myself, "What the fuck! Does no one have any respect for this peaceful moment?" Hell all I wanted was a moment to enjoy the outdoors at Manoa Valley in peace and quiet. Soldiers with PTSD just want peace and quiet, which is why most of us stay at home and regain our peacefulness through our own surroundings.

Waianae Coast

As the months went on and we continued our field trips, we paid a visit to this hospital that didn't look like a hospital. It sat on the side of the mountain facing the Waianae Coast. All I wanted to do was sit out on the patio and watch the ocean waves. I could sit there and watch the ocean well after sundown while sitting on the mountain. I wished there could be a moment where time stood still, and the peaceful moments would last for eternity. Moments like this would put me into a better mood. I listened to Sade in the evenings and Sean Paul in the daytime. His music would bring out the island's smooth vibe to where everything was slow and easy, and every day was happy hour all day. I guess, in my life, I just want those Sade and Sean Paul vibes all day, every day. Their music helps my mind go easy like Sunday morning.

Conducting Homework Outing

During each outing, we would talk about our events during our group session the day after. One of our counselors mentioned that we should go out on our own to do outings. There had been times when I left our group sessions at noon because I felt so motivated and uplifted. I took huge steps to go downtown to Ala Moana Mall. This mall takes up a little over six city blocks. A lot of tourists go to this mall and it's constantly busy. I started out going to the mall for lunch. While purchasing my lunch, I found myself in the hypervigilant mode because tons of people were walking around.

When I sat outside on the bench, this guy came up and asked me if he could sit on the bench with me. I said sure. As I watched from the corner of my right eye, I noticed he laid his backpack down on the bench and walked away. I quickly turned around and before I could say anything, I noticed that he only took two steps and put a few items in the nearby trashcan. I almost lost control of myself. I guess my hypervigilance had me so keyed up because that reminded me of too many things that happened in Iraq. Someone would leave their backpack on a bench or in a building and have the bag blow up, causing damage and death. Like I said before, we Soldiers treat everyone as a potential threat.

After lunch, I went to the main part of the mall to do window shopping, looking at every person who walked by. Two hours went by and I was ready to head home to west side of the island, but I had one problem: I was so keyed up and hypervigilant that I couldn't remember where I parked my truck. I spent another two hours walking and looking for my truck. I was so frustrated that my head started to hurt; I felt like I was about to have a nervous breakdown. My mind ran a hundred miles a minute and my heart was racing.

That's when I knew I had to have someone with me at all times when I was out in public.

The next day was our field trip day. I told my buddy what happened at the mall. I told him I still treated people as a threat, and I just didn't trust anyone out in public, even after we had spent a few months on these outings. He mentioned to me that he was having the same issues. We didn't know what to do. I told him there was no problem with us feeling or acting the way we did; it was the civilians who were acting so carefree as if nothing would ever happen to them. At the same time I said that, we were in the van with the radio on and we heard that there was a bombing during the Boston Marathon. We both locked eyes and said, "What the fuck?" That attack just confirmed why we as combat Vets stayed hypervigilant and treated everyone as a threat. I believed our guards would never go down.

History of Shell
Shock and Family Reintegration

After eight months of learning about our issues with PTSD in our group session, I wanted to learn how the struggle of PTSD and family reintegration affected Soldiers from the past wars. I did this because soon enough, I would have to reintegrate with my family. I was away from my wife and daughter for about over a year while my treatment for PTSD was going on.

I learned that in the past wars, the name they used was "shell shock," which is today known as PTSD. Soldiers in the past wars described combat as an image of a nightmare from hell where all decency and humanity could be lost. For men who fought under these conditions, coming home was a very difficult transition. The difficult task of transition has turned out to be harder to obtain than first expected. Problems ranging from the availability of jobs in the workforce to raising a child and post-traumatic stress would make this return to "normalcy" an uneasy task. This explains why Soldiers today would rather be in Iraq or Afghanistan, because after being in combat, war has become normal.

One of the major problems that Soldiers faced upon their return to the States was the availability of jobs. I learned during World War II, the United States government encouraged 1.3 million women with husbands in the service to enter the workforce as well as the minorities, along with the a migration of African-American workers from the South to fill the wartime need for labor.

My understanding of the history of American black men from the Southern states was that to have a place in the workplace was a slap in the face. What I mean is, it was okay for African American men to be accepted in these industrial jobs that the average white man would have taken, but since most of the white men went off to war, that tells me that employing a black man was the only option left to keep these industrial companies. But if the war wasn't going on, these industrial companies, or any company for that matter, would not be likely to give any black men the time of day. Yet all black men needed a job to put food on the table for their families, just like any other average white man.

The reason why I felt so bitter about employing black men as the last resort is because I saw myself that way: not having a job in America after military service. In others words, I did my job well during my four tours in Iraq, but at the same time, it also felt like I was only good enough to do my job as a Construction Engineer when my life was on the line. Now that I was home in the States with tons of experience, do you think any company would give me the time of day? Hell, I couldn't get a job at the Department of Transportation (DOT) in Honolulu, even though I had experience in fixing roads that had been damaged by IEDs in Iraq. At that time in Hawaii, they spent several months working on the H1 (freeway) doing road repairs during the weeknights. I could go to Iraq, have my life on the line, and do road repairs after roadside bombing "IED" went off destroying the roads that we used for delivering supplies to various camp sites, but I couldn't work for the DOT based on my road repair experience throughout Iraq.

Another anxiety Soldiers faced were the reactions of the children they left behind. Most of the fathers that returned from war became concerned with how they would fit into the family system. Some fathers were determined to take an active role in the family, and they did by becoming the master disciplinarians. Returning fathers came home to find undisciplined and unruly children, a far cry from the ordered military life they had led during the war.

My Experience

I saw these problems when I flew from Hawaii to Utah for Christmas to be with my wife and daughter. I first noticed that they were both independent and they had their own routine. My wife was never a needy type to where she couldn't do anything or function without her husband. It felt like I wasn't needed at the house and that they could function well without me. I remember telling my daughter, age fourteen, to clean her room because I thought her room was dirty. My wife intervened, saying that she cleaned her room just the other day. I knew right then and there that I really didn't have a say or, should I say, I chose to give up that right to have a say because I didn't want to lose control of my anger and blow up at my wife over a dirty bedroom and ruin Christmas with my family. It almost felt as if I had to put on this pretend happy face around my family.

More History Lessons

Most wives and children noticed behavioral changes in their men before and after the war. Veterans returning from the battlefield would suffer nightmares and flashbacks of combat, triggering alienation and loneliness, desperation and withdrawal. This increased alcoholism among the returning Soldiers and led to an increase in the number of divorces that occurred after the war. From my experience, I never turned to alcohol or drugs. I believe what helped me was doing kitchen remodels and bathroom remodels on the island of Oahu on the weekends. Normally, the weekends were the time when Soldiers with PTSD got into trouble because they have had a lot of time on their hands to think. The emotional effects from war will come crashing down on you, and that is how drugs and alcohol come to play for most Soldiers. With my changes of behavior after the war, I don't understand why my wife is still with me today. I've always wondered if it is because she hopes that the old me, prior to September 11, 2001, will come back? I don't know; I have never asked her. But I am fighting to have the new me, and hopefully I can help someone else become a better person.

The return home for many Soldiers was not at all comfortable. After fighting under unbearable conditions for years, the return to domestic life was undoubtedly not what was expected. With the problems of finding work and those encountered in family dynamics, this reintegration was anything but smooth. From what I learned about the history of shell shock, we, as combat Vets, have gone through the same shit after every war. What I'm so surprised about is that the military and our government have not done anything for the Vietnam War Vets, Korean War Vets, and the World War II Vets. I know from previous Vietnam Vets, that they were told to shut up and never talk about the war to anyone. And that's the wrong answer.

Those Vets spent years of not saying anything, emotions stayed trapped inside, and the memories of events kept replaying in their heads.

From my experience, this is why providing work for US Veterans is so important, because having steady work does help with some of our PTSD issues. At times when I come home at the end of the day, I'm normally too tired to think about my issues, so I just shower, eat, and go to bed.

I also learned firsthand at age eighteen, when I worked in the foundry with my dad in Oakland, California, the rate of employment there was about 70 percent Veterans, and most were retired Navy, as well Army and Marines. They all served in Vietnam at one point of time or another, so they all had that war mind-set as far as getting shit done and providing the best quality of work one can put out.

The company had a large contract with the Navy to make parts for their battleships that were docked at Alameda Naval Air Station. Back then, these Veterans worked extremely hard and maintained their military work ethic. If I was two seconds too slow on getting my job done, they were all over my ass to pick up the pace. In other words, as young man, I had to work by their standards. The sad thing even back then was that I knew something was wrong with them by the looks in their eyes. Yes, some had a little drink of alcohol on the job so they could contain their anger and rage from the Vietnam War. Upper management of the company didn't bother them too much because they got their job done, which meant the company made money.

As time went on, I heard stories of how some of the guys felt all they did was work hard and come home to drink until they passed out. The memories from war may have appeared, but alcohol and/or drugs took away the pain momentarily. Most families just left them alone and allowed them to do their thing, but I can figure out that they might not have been the best father for their kids. I can honestly say, however, that they never missed a day of work because of their PTSD, and that is why I believe that having a steady job is therapy for PTSD. At the same time, there are not that many foundry businesses going on in today's world.

Most of the jobs are computer jobs, and most of us combat Veterans are not the types that like to sit down and look at a computer screen for eight hours and drink Starbucks coffee all damn day. Somehow I wish our government could bring back the old school industrial jobs like the foundries, steel mills, and the Navy shipyards, where a blue collar worker can work hard, put food on the table, and put money away for their kid's college instead of looking for ways to cut our military and retirement benefits.

Remember, work is therapy and with a little improvement on mental health treatments, we, as Soldiers, can be productive Veterans in society and not damaged goods. Establishing a Wounded Warrior Transition Battalion through different duty stations is a good start because of the treatment I've received for PTSD. I don't know where I would be in life if it weren't for the WBT at Schofield Barracks. However, with that said, that doesn't mean I'm cured of PTSD. What I'm saying is that I'm fully educated through my group sessions, and I have learned the tools that I can use if I'm having a bad day out in public. I have come to terms that I will have good days and bad days. I also came to terms that my patience is very short on stupidity amongst people, but I do try to keep those people far away from me. The bottom line is that I have to take it one day at a time until I can learn to put that battle mind-set to rest, let my guard down, and not look at people as potential threats.

Retirement

Yes, I can say—hallelujah!—the United States Army has given me something that all Soldiers have been looking for after they put in some serious time in like I have: our freedom papers, known as "Retirement Orders." It took me ten months of being in the Wounded Warrior Transition Battalion (WTB) and a total of five years fighting for and getting treatment for PTSD. As I mentioned earlier in this book, I had been fighting to get help since November 2009, and at this point my retirement date was 22 November 2013 with seventeen years of service. I figure spending six years running back and forth to Iraq, from January 2003 to November 2009, doing construction missions in different parts of the world, it was time for SSG Duckworth to retire. When you see my military history, you will see why I was looking forward to retirement.

Military History

- Enlisted in The United States Army (November 1996)
- Duty Stations: Fort Wainwright, Alaska; Fort Sill, Oklahoma; Schofield Barracks, Hawaii.
- Military Occupational Specialty (MOS) 12 Hotel Construction Supervisor.
- Rank: Staff Sergeant (SSG), Retired E-6
- Construction Engineer/Construction Supervisor

Construction Missions

- Four tours in Iraq (January 2003 to November 2009)
- Two tours in Marshall Islands (Kwajalien 1998, 2000)
- Three tours in Thailand (1999, 2007, 2008) Cobra Gold
- Two tours to American Samoa (2011, 2012)

US Army Awards

- One Meritorious Service Medal
- Three Army Commendation Medals
- Five Army Achievement Medals
- One Combat Action Badge

When you hear about a Soldier retiring, most people think retired Veterans receive everything under the sun relating to medical benefits for themselves and their family, as well as retirement pay. Well, when you do a medical retirement process, it seems like an uphill battle to make sure your benefits and other compensation falls in place. I will explain later on what I mean about an uphill battle regarding fighting for your benefits, but let's just say fighting for your benefits is like winning a small battle in Iraq.

Retirement Benefits

When Soldiers like me are medically retired due to PTSD, we have to be retired under a certain status called Temporary Duty Retirement List (TDRL). It seems like this is another way the Army can still have you by the balls by being on TDRL status. TDRL is a list of Army members found to be unfit for performance of military duties by reason of physical disability, which may be permanent, but has not sufficiently stabilized to permit an accurate assessment of a permanent degree of disability. The Secretary of the Army is required, by law, to maintain the TDRL and has delegated responsibility for this function to headquarters at the United States Army Physical Disability Agency (USAPDA).

Another part of the TDRL status is that in order to check to see if your condition has stabilized, by law the USAPDA has to reevaluate the Soldier every eighteen months up to five years. This is the part where I thought the Army would retire a Soldier, but at the same time, they still have the Soldier under their control, which means they still have him by the chain. With my case (being retired due to PTSD), I was permanently retired eighteen months later on June 6, 2014. Since my PTSD has stabilized, the Army has considered me 50 percent disabled, for which I get to keep my medical benefits for my family and me.

During those eighteen months, I wasn't sitting around waiting for things to fall out of the sky and for everything to be perfect—this is the part where you have to fight and protect your benefits and keep a watchful eye on how your retirement benefits play out. In other words, these are the battles you have to face while maintaining or protecting your benefits. In my case, I had to listen to what guidelines the Army JAG lawyer gave me after reviewing my medical board evaluation. Guidelines were to place myself into another group session relating to PTSD through the VA. My first thought was, *Damn, I'm about to go through another emotional roller coaster ride in PTSD group sessions.* For several days, I kept thinking about the whole ordeal and about taking up more of my personal time going through another group session when I should be looking for another career or job after retirement. But the more I kept thinking about it, I realized I was still thinking like a Soldier. *Hey, I have already been through the group session. I'm ready to face society.* But what I was doing was being like a Soldier trying to suck it up and drive on, knowing there were other issues hanging over me, but that I couldn't put a label on them. When March 2013 came around, I finally transitioned to Utah to be with my family and enrolled myself in PTSD group counseling called Cognitive Processing Therapy (CPT). Another group session I was involved in was Veterans of Color—and there's a story behind that. Let's just say I was at the VA in Salt Lake City three times a week for over twelve weeks, so looking for a job was out of the question because there was no way any employer would allow a new employee to take that much time off from work to attend to their group session. This was the part where I had to give up a lot of things like having job and having extra income. If I had a job and chose not to focus on further treatment, then there was a chance that I might lose my retirement benefits altogether. So again, it was like an uphill battle fighting for my benefits.

Combat-Related Special Compensation (CRSC)

Combat-Related Special Compensation is another form of benefit you are entitled to when you are medically retired. CRSC is a monthly entitlement that allows eligible military retirees to recover some or all of their retired pay that was offset by their Department of Veterans Affairs (VA) disability compensation. Eligible retirees must have a combat-related injury and may receive this entitlement in addition to any retired pay they receive from the Defense Finance and Accounting Service (DFAS). This was how CRSC worked for me and, yes, you can get the whole packet ready with your:

- DD form 2860
- Retirement orders
- VA rating (Disability Evaluation System Rating Decision)
- DA Form 199
- DA Form 2173
- DA Form 3349
- All your deployment orders to Iraq or Afghanistan

You can't turn in your packet until you have received your first VA compensation. My first VA check didn't come in until March 2014 and, during that same week, I mailed off the whole packet to DFAS, but I received a regular retirement check from the Army until the VA compensation kicked in. Then I had to wait until July 1, 2014, for the CRSC compensation to kick in. While I waited for four months, the VA took half my pay because they found out I was accepting VA compensation while I was in the US Army Reserves doing my weekend drills. I was not aware I couldn't do this. Luckily, I paid it all back and then I was able to receive my full VA compensation on July 1, right along with my first CRSC compensation.

I have to say, living off of half of VA pay for four months was pretty hard. It was just enough to pay rent and child support. After that, there was only enough money for gas to make it to my VA appointment four times a week. Now that all the financial hardship was out of the way, I could enjoy the VA and CRSC compensation at $2,945 a month. Now, only if I could find another career.

Like I said before, watching out for benefits and additional treatments was really a full-time job. I don't see how other Veterans can have forty-hour-a-week jobs, seek additional treatment for PTSD, and constantly follow up on their compensations. Between receiving my permanently retired orders, VA compensation, and CRSC compensation, it felt like I had won the war against the United States Army.

Keep in mind, back in December 2010, when I got out of active duty, I was so angry about how the United States Army had treated me. I was planning on getting out and saying, "Fuck it, I don't want anything to do with the Army." I didn't want to see anything that reminded me of the Army, but I had to listen to someone who knew me very well, pulled me aside, and said, "Duck, don't give the Army the satisfaction." What my buddy meant was, "Don't throw all your benefits away like that. You have worked too damn hard for the Army, and it's time for the Army to take care of you." With all that said, someone else told me to join the Army Reserves, even though my PTSD was kicking in. I had an ounce of good sense in me to listen to my battle buddies, so look at me now. Five years later, I'm retired. Thank you, Jesus.

Double Dipping

I received a letter from Veterans Affairs (24march 2014) saying that they noticed I was accepting VA compensation while I was doing my weekend drill pay during the fiscal year of 2012. So the thing that bothered me the most was when I left active duty 20 December 2010, during the first week of January 2011, I submitted all of my medical documents to the VA to start the process for my compensation of fourteen years of active-duty service. That same month, I decided to go into the Army Reserves (9th TSG Theater Support Group) at Fort Shafter in Hawaii. When I was processed into the unit, the VA claims were in processing, and at the same time as I was being processed; no one ever asked me if I had a VA claim or if I would be receiving any VA compensation in the near future.

One year had passed and I started receiving VA compensation. I attended all my weekend drills. Between the weekend drills pay ($650 a month) and the monthly compensation ($750), that was the only source of income I had at that time. I had a difficult time finding a full-time job to support my family. We lived in a state where the cost of living was really high.

Thanks to the chain of command at the 9th TSG, they had been withholding valuable information about collecting VA compensation while collecting drill pay. I believe that should be the first question they ask when they receive Soldiers from active duty to Reserves. I owed $3,000 to the VA all because of a valuable question they didn't ask me, and now I had to pay for it. Now that I'm medically retired, it took the VA almost three years to inform me that I had to repay half my compensation while conducting weekend drill pay (one weekend a month). I was told that I was "double dipping." With the troubles I went through with low income and fighting for benefits I was entitled to, let's shine some light on double standards and

147

"double dipping" amongst federal employees. According to reporter Shane Goldmacher, writing for the news site *Government Executive*, nearly one in five members of Congress collects a government pension on top of his or her $174,000 salary. Perfectly legal, this "double dipping" amounts to $3.6 million in public retirement funds in 2012. A Democratic Representative from Ohio pocketed $253,323 from his pension. With his congressional salary, he earned more than President Obama. A Republican Representative from New York, on the other hand, said he wrote a check to the US Treasury to cover his military pension, minus taxes owed. "We did not want to double dip on the taxpayers," he said. These Congressmen and women are abusing their power by writing their own rules and allowing themselves to "double dip."

Meanwhile, half of my compensation was being taken away to pay back something that happened almost four years ago. The slow service of the VA causes Veterans to be one step away from being homeless. I only had enough money to pay my rent and child support. I'm just glad I was living in Utah and paying rent of $1,050 a month for a five-bedroom place. If I was in Hawaii, I would be the homeless Veteran living on the beach. I just have one question for Congress: can I have a job in Washington so I can double dip like the rest of you?

Another problem I discovered with the VA was that I had received another letter on that stated, word for word, "We received information from the defense manpower data center (DMDC) that you returned to active duty on 21 September 2012 through 15 November, 2013. Your awards were not adjusted to reflect your return to active duty on 21 September 2012. A Veteran may not receive VA benefits while on active duty. Therefore, we propose to stop VA compensation payments." I just want to say that I was put back on active duty to receive treatment for PTSD through the Soldier Transition Battalion at Schofield Barracks in Hawaii. During the first five days I was in transitioning into the Wounded Warrior Transition Battalion, I managed to break away to take my active-duty orders to the VA so they could stop my compensation. Two months went by and I received a billing from the Department of Veterans Affairs Debt Management Center stating that the VA paid me benefits to which I was not entitled. The bill was for $1.062.67.

I didn't have the money during the month of December to pay it back, but I did pay the VA bill in full in March of 2013 with a cashier's check. Hell, I even took a picture of the cashier's check just so I would have it for my record. It's a damn shame that when it came to paying back the government, or the VA, I was down to taking pictures of payment just to cover my ass. I tried to do the right thing by turning in my active-duty orders to stop my VA compensation, but I still got screwed over. It was like, "Damned if you do, damned if you don't." I believed Veterans shouldn't have to pay back shit if the VA system was that damn slow. Their slowness disrupts Veterans' financial matters, especially if that's their only income.

Medical Benefits

I just want to share how happy I am to be retired and have medical benefits for my family. When I enrolled my family into Tricare Prime, I paid $546 for the whole year. I paid for the whole year because I wasn't sure how my finances were going to be through the year of 2014. Now I'm glad I did that because I lost half my VA compensation due to the drama in 2012, I wasn't able to afford my dental plan so I lost the dental plan for my family.

Shortly after I rejoined my family in Utah, my wife needed surgery. After all these years in the Army, my wife never needed any type of surgery, but 120 days after retirement, she needed surgery. Funny how that works out. During the days of my wife's surgery, we had to pay a co-pay of $25. When we got ready to pay, it ended up being $17 at a civilian hospital. Another lady needed the same surgery as my wife and she had to pay a $1,800 co-pay. I had to thank God I was retired with good benefits, which meant I was not forced into Obama Care or any other medical care that's out there. Somehow I needed to get back on track with the dental plan. I did try to pay the dental plan for the whole year, but they wouldn't accept it.

More Group Sessions

Cognitive Processing Therapy

Cognitive therapy is a behavioral treatment for Post-Traumatic Stress Disorder and related problems. CPT is designed to help improve PTSD symptoms and associated symptoms, such as depression, anxiety, guilt, and shame. CPT helps identify and explore how different traumas have changed thoughts and beliefs and how some of these ways of thinking may keep a person stuck in their symptoms.

My Stuck Points

Veterans with PTSD find themselves holding a strong belief about why the trauma happens to them. Here are a few examples of my "stuck" points:

No Civilian Can Understand Me

I believe that civilians will never understand a combat Veteran. The civilian ways of thinking are carefree with a wide range of gray areas on why jobs or tasks don't get done on time or why they can't be where they are supposed to be on time. A Veteran's mind-set is black and white with no gray areas. In other words, we know it's very important to be where we supposed to be on time. If not, we could cause our battle buddies to get killed on the battlefield. Some civilian workers think it's okay to be thirty minutes late for work, and that's wrong if you ask me. Coming in late like that tells me that a civilian is unreliable and untrustworthy.

Combat Veterans understand how important it is to get the job done to the fullest. One of the seven Army Core Values is "Selfless Service," which means you put the welfare of the nation, the Army, and your subordinates before your own. The bottom line is that it's your duty to get the job done no matter what. I've heard stories about

151

how some civilian workers would leave work early—because their child had a football game or something like that—knowing they were behind on work. If you ask me, damn those football games! When you work as a group, that means you work as a team and get caught up with your work. Last time I checked, the company is paying your weekly wages, which means you have a job that helps you put food on the table for your family, not your child's football games.

Another thing that some civilians don't understand about me is certain meaning of words. For example, if a civilian would say, "Gee it's hot today. It's ninety degrees outside." My true understanding of hot is 130 degrees in Iraq with full gear on, working twelve- to fifteen-hour days getting shit done.

When someone says, "I'm hungry," I just want to say, "You're hungry because you have not eaten in three hours." My understanding of hunger is I have not eaten in the past ten hours, and I have been working for the past twelve hours. There have been times when I did jobs like a kitchen remodel and the only thing I would eat is a Snickers bar and a Pepsi at seven in the morning. That would be all I ate that day. When 6:30 p.m. came around, I was done for the day and ready to eat. I believe a lot of that has to do with my selfless service of putting the mission first before my needs. Another part of the seven Army Core Values is "Duty," meaning to fulfill your obligations. Doing your duty means more than carrying out your assigned tasks. I carried the seven Army Core Values even when I did my side jobs.

I Must Be on Guard at All Times

After multiple tours in Iraq and seeing so many things happen, I couldn't help but be on guard, always looking for potential threats. The insurgents in Iraq did not have uniforms on, so we as Soldiers could not see the difference between friend and enemy. Look at what happened at the Boston Marathon in 2013 with a roadside bombing as the race went on. After seeing the video before the attack, I noticed something odd about the guy: he was carrying a backpack. The sad thing is the average civilian didn't catch it because they were in a carefree mind-set. Basically, I must stay on guard because the threat can come from anywhere. Furthermore, if I'm out in public with friends and family members, as a Soldier, I must protect them with my life at all times.

Another reason I must protect them with my life is the Oath of Enlistment: "I, Jocephus Josey Duckworth, do solemnly swear that I will support and defend the Constitution of the United States against all enemies, foreign and domestic." There is more to the Oath of Enlistment, but the most important statement for me is to fight against all enemies, foreign and domestic. This tells me the Oath of Enlistment won't expire until I leave this earth, and that is why it so important for me to protect my friends and family against all enemies, foreign and domestic.

Another reason why I need to be on guard is because of the school shootings that have been carrying on for the past ten years. With all the school teachers and principals who work every day, you mean to tell me they didn't know that student was crazy? I mean a student just doesn't wake up and decide he is going to shoot up the school. Most of these shootings have been planned out for weeks or months, which means the behavior has changed, but no staff member caught that. That tells me that every staff member comes to school with that carefree mind-set. One of the ways to solve the school shootings is to hire combat Vets as school teachers, janitors, or undercover security personnel. We are always hypervigilant, and we can see the threats before they even happen. And if it does happen, we would see to it that the threats got taken out, even it called for putting our lives on the line to save the innocent students. Most schools won't hire combat Vets because we have PTSD.

I Must Responds to All Threats with Force

With my combat mind-set that won't shut off, I must respond to all threats with force, especially when it comes to protecting innocent people, my family, and friends. Visiting my hometown of Oakland, California, makes me want to carry a civilian version of the M4 with a basic load of 210 rounds that consist of seven magazines with thirty rounds each. With random shootings in the "hood" and bad drug deals that go wrong, I have no choice but to carry my M4 as if I'm in Iraq while visiting or living in Oakland. The difference between my weapon and the drug dealer's or a gangster's weapon is that I know how to zero my weapon. Every Soldier who has spent some time at the shooting range zeroing their weapon to get a tight shot group on a target knows what the fuck I'm talking about. "One shot, one kill." These thugs and drug dealers just know how to pull the trigger and pray that their bullet catches the person they're trying to hit, but they end up hitting a little toddler or innocent bystander who had nothing to do with the situation.

Other People Should Not Be Trusted

From my personal experience with civilians, I don't trust most civilians the same way I trust my fellow Soldiers who served with me throughout years. I trust my fellow Soldiers, I know they have my back, and I will have theirs in the time of war. I know my fellow Soldiers are trained very well in their jobs, and I know things will get done. I know my fellow Soldiers will save my life just as I will save theirs. As a retired Veteran, I feel like a fish out of water living among civilians. In the workforce, I can't trust them to do their jobs and be team players, which means all they worry about is themselves or getting off work early because of their children's after-school activities or the desire to go golfing. Most civilians would rather use their phones to video an elderly woman get beat by some young punk—and have the balls to put it on social media like it was cool—than put their phones down and stop the beating. A combat Vet would have kicked some ass and protected the elderly woman and proceeded to get medical help. I can trust civilians to worry about their Starbucks coffee being made right. I can trust parents to be best friends with their children because parents today have lost the true meaning of the authority role of being a parent to a child, meaning parents don't understand that they're the law of their household. Don't be afraid to tell your child no. Or don't be afraid to put that belt to the child's ass when needed. Don't show weakness because when you do, you just lose complete control of your child, and that's why kids today have such disrespect toward their parents and people with authority. I can trust civilians to worry about their own useless lives and their kids' activities. Bottom line: I can trust civilians to live in their own small-minded lives and play the time-out game with their children, knowing that crap doesn't work.

The Government Can't Be Trusted

Since I'm retired, I still feel like someone is out to get me. Who? Congress (the House Budget Committee). It's funny how in the United States, the Armed Forces only make up 1 percent of the population, and the House Budget Committee wants to cut our pension. I can tell you this, Congress: keep in mind, that we, as trained Veterans, are trained to fight and survive in combat. So, Congress, I'm asking you, are you trained and ready to go to war with us Veterans? It would make more sense to cut out welfare. In fact, do the math on the percentage of lazy ass Americans that are on welfare, riding the system so they don't have to work. Here's the deal that was made by Congress and the Department of Defense. They have to follow the rules. As the code is currently written, service members can be eligible for early retirement if it is determined that, due to a physical disability, that individual is no longer able to perform the duties of their office, grade, or rank. The individual must hold a disability rating of 30 percent or more, according to Department of Defense standards, and the disability must be the proximate result of performing their duties during a time of war or national emergency. A Republican told *The Weekly Standard* that the changes are appropriate because servicemen and women who retire in their forties, after serving for two decades, are still young enough to maintain a job. Reporter John McCormack quotes Congressman Ryan in his article, "Ryan Defends Reduction to Cost-of-Living Adjustments for Early Military Retirees" (December 15, 2013). "We give them a slightly smaller adjustment for inflation because they're still in their working years and in most cases, earning another paycheck."

This motherfucker doesn't understand that there's an agreement from our government to tell us young men and women that if we join any four branches of service and give our country twenty years of service, the United States government will give you full retirement and medical benefits, which means if a young man or woman joins the military at the age of eighteen and gives the government twenty years, then he or she will retire at age thirty-eight.

That Republican does not understand that we work ten times harder than an average man or woman. I completed four tours to Iraq conducting construction missions. I performed my job at 110 percent for six years in Iraq. I've done construction projects in different parts of the world. Now that I'm physically injured and still having PTSD issues after months of treatment, I just want to say that I'm done with working at the age of forty-two. With my injuries, I need to work at my own pace, and there's no company that will allow us Vets to work at our own pace, unless we have a government-status position, or a GS job. But wait, our government is not hiring any Vets!

It is hard to work in the civilian sector when you still carry the seven Army Core Values or living with the highest standards. In having the Army Core Values after military service and trying to have a regular job, you will find yourself bumping heads with the civilian workforce. As a Soldier you can't just drop the Army Core Values like a bad habit. It's in you for life. I believe our attributes in leadership as well as being Soldiers and getting things done are ways to advance the civilian workforce. Here are some examples of what we are trained to do in a leadership position:

1. Accelerated Learning Curve

- Veterans have the proven ability to learn new skills and concepts.
- Veterans can enter the workforce with identifiable and transferable skills, proven in real-world situations.

2. Leadership

- The military trains service members to lead by example, as well as through direction, delegation, motivation, and inspiration.
- Successful Veterans have learned to trust and obey the commands of their superiors.
- Veterans with sterner stiff will ask questions and can still think on their own.
- Veterans understand that a team needs a leader to achieve a vision.

3. Teamwork

- Veterans understand how genuine teamwork grows out of a responsibility to one's colleagues.
- Veterans who have undergone the most demanding training or actual missions know that a good team distributes the workload and plays to the strengths and talents of each team member.
- Veterans know what real teamwork looks like and find it easy to listen and communicate with others.

4. Commitment

- Veterans have sacrificed their own wants and needs for the greater good.
- Veterans understand commitment and what it takes to succeed.
- Veterans have the experience and character to fulfill this much-needed trait in the workplace.

5. Efficient Performance under Pressure

- Veterans understand the rigors of tight schedules and limited resources.

- Veterans have developed the capacity to know how to accomplish priorities on time, in spite of tremendous stress.
- They know the critical importance of staying with a task until it is done right.

6. Respect for Procedures

- Veterans have gained a unique perspective on the value of accountability.
- Veterans can grasp their place within an organizational framework, becoming responsible for subordinates' actions to higher supervisory levels.
- They know how policies and procedures enable an organization to exist.

7. Integrity

- Veterans know what it means to do "an honest day's work."
- Prospective employers can take advantage of a track record of integrity, often including security clearances.
- Integrity translates into qualities of sincerity and trustworthiness.

8. Conscious of Health and Safety Standards

- Thanks to extensive training, Veterans are aware of health and safety protocols both for themselves and the welfare of others.
- Veterans represent a drug-free workforce that is aware of maintaining personal health and fitness.
- At company level, their awareness and conscientiousness translate into protection of employees, property, and materials.

Looking at civilian workers, I've seen some piss-poor working standards from the management on down. The civilian workforce doesn't know anything about the words "Loyalty," "Duty," "Respect," "Selfless Service," "Honor," "Integrity," and "Personal Courage." So as a retired combat Vet with PTSD and other health issues, I just don't have time for bullshit in the civilian workforce. From what I've experienced in the civilian workforce, there's no loyalty from the employee to the company and there's no loyalty from the company to the employee. So with that being said, there's no trust, no teamwork, and everyone is out for themselves. In a combat zone, we, as Soldiers, don't play those games. It can cost us our lives when we don't have teamwork, trust, and loyalty. The mission doesn't get accomplished.

Mistakes Are Intolerable and Cause Serious Harm or Death

I know I can't stand any mistakes. For instance, I treat all my personal vehicles like my military vehicles. I make sure all tires and brakes are in good shape, and the oil is changed as necessary. Basically I just want all my vehicles at the ready for long road trips just like all our military vehicles are ready for the next convoy mission. When it comes to people doing stupid shit, it really pisses me off. Like in Hawaii, I'm so tired of these so-called accidental drownings of young kids. My question is, where in the fuck are the parents? Hell, my daughter is fourteen years old and a better swimmer than I am, but guess what? When we are in the water, I'm one arm's length from her. When these parents lose their children due to drowning and lack of parenting skills, they don't deserve to be parents. Sometimes I wish I could grab those useless parents, strap them down to a table, blindfold them, and pour five-gallon buckets of water over their noses and mouths just to give them the feeling of drowning and being hopeless, and I will keep doing that until I get tired.

Another issue I have with most parents is I'm sick of hearing about them leaving their kids in the car with the windows rolled up while shopping on a hot summer day. My question is, how are you so busy that you can't look in the back of your car to see if your child is back there? I bet they made sure they brought their iPhone and their smoothie drink into the store, but they couldn't take two seconds to see if their child was in the car. I just want to say, people stop doing dumb shit that causes death.

Expressing Any Emotion
Means I Will Lose Control of Me

Most of the time, I have to just bite my tongue and just let it be. People just don't understand the way a combat mind works and how deep Soldiers' emotions are. It's just like me trying to figure out what it feels like to give birth.

Pattern of Problematic Thinking

The pattern of problematic thinking often becomes habitual thoughts that cause us to engage in self-defeating behavior. As you read along, I will share some samples of my pattern of problematic thinking.

<u>Jumping to a conclusion when evidence is lacking or even contradictory</u>

When I visit Oakland to pick up my truck from the shipping port, I notice corner stores and cheap motels throughout the Bay Area, and I find myself enraged with the people working or owning these corner stores and cheap hotels. It's because most of the owners are from the Arabic region (Iraq, Afghanistan, Pakistan, Iran). I wonder how in the hell they have the balls to come into my country and start a business?

My other thinking is how much of their profits are going back to their homeland to fund other terrorist groups to buy weapons to kill my fellow Soldiers and Marines in Iraq and Afghanistan or plan another attack on US soil?

Another thing I think about is our government looking over their spending habits. What people don't understand is that terrorist groups are like drug dealers. If they can use you for their personal gain, they will. In other words, if a terrorist group finds a businessman who's from the Middle East and owns a business in the United States, that business owner now works for the terrorist group, which means a certain percentage of the profits go to the terrorist group to fund their next terrorist attack. If the businessman doesn't comply with the terrorist, the businessman and the rest of his family's heads will be cut off. So if the businessman loves his family, he will give up a portion of his profits to save his family. Meanwhile, the average American citizen just walks into the store and buys what they want and never gives it a thought about if their money is going toward terrorist groups. Yes, I know that is a long and deep thought, but that's on my mind when I see stores and cheap motels being run by someone from the Arabic region.

Exaggerating or minimizing a situation

I guess the people at the McDonald's that I go to in Kapolei have seen the PTSD side of me. I went to McDonald's around ten to get a burger. I decided to go the bathroom first to wash my hands. When I entered the bathroom, I saw a guy with a red hat and red shirt. My first thought was, *There's something wrong with him; he looks a little funny.* I continued to wash my hands. When I was done, I took a step back to turn around to dry my hands, and all I saw was what I thought was a dead body lying on the nasty floor. I rushed out into the lobby and gave an order to the McDonald's staff to dial 911 because there was a body lying on the floor in the men's bathroom.

Of course, everyone looked at me stupidly so I grabbed my phone and was about to dial 911. The manager came to the front counter. I told her she needed to check the bathroom because there was a body on the floor. At the same time, I saw that same guy with the red shirt and red hat, and I asked him who that person was on bathroom floor. He told me it was his girlfriend; she was passed out drunk on the floor. Then I asked him what the fuck she was doing in the men's bathroom. I told him to get his girlfriend out of the men's bathroom and take her ass home. The manager looked at me strangely, said she was passed out drunk, and kept walking toward the back of the store.

So I guess never mind that there was a woman in the men's bathroom, and I was the last black guy in the bathroom. I have to say that event scared me so badly that I ate my burger in my truck instead of in the lobby, like I always did. It took me about twenty-four hours to calm down. People don't understand us war Veterans who have been back and forth to Iraq and seen so much bad shit happen. Just like I saw a seven-year-old Iraqi girl who was shot in the head but still alive. It is no joke when you see a body lying on the floor motionless. It is not an everyday thing to go into a public restroom to wash your hands only to see a body lying on a nasty ass bathroom floor.

Three days later, I went back to that same McDonald's and I saw the same manager in the parking lot. I said, "Ma'am, I'm sorry for the way I acted on Friday night." She was standoffish, like she was scared of me. She walked away from me saying, "Yeah, okay." At the same time, she had that look like, *Hey, let me hurry up and get inside the restaurant because of this crazy Veteran.*

After that, I felt ashamed of my actions at this McDonald's that I had been going to four times a week. I allowed them to see the worst side of me. All I tried to do was report a body lying on the floor and inform the shift manager of the situation in the bathroom. Later that week, I saw the main manager and asked her if she knew what had happened that Friday night. She said no, so I told her the story. She was in shock that the night manager didn't give her a brief on what went on during her shift. That just gave me another reason why I can't trust managers to take their position seriously.

Veterans of Color

Veterans of Color is a fairly new group session at the VA in Salt Lake City, Utah. The group session gives a voice to the African-American men and women who have served in America's Armed Forces, sharing history of heroic service from Soldiers of all ranks and stature who had to conquer the enemy while battling for equality.

I understand that back between World War II and the Vietnam War, black service members had the two toughest jobs: fighting for America's freedom and fighting for equality within the ranks of the each black service member's chain of command. Now, I'm not going to say there wasn't any lack of equality throughout my years of service, but there is a true lack of equality after military service. One of the problems I've seen (but didn't know there was a label for it) is called "racial battle fatigue." I learned that racial battle fatigue is no different than battling combat stress in the battlefield, which leads to PTSD.

There is constant racial battle fatigue while adjusting to civilian life. Dealing with racial battle fatigue on a daily basis can lead to another psychological illness called generalized anxiety disorder, which leads to chronic worrying, intrusive thoughts, and difficulty concentrating. From what I've learned in our group session, racial battle fatigue and generalized anxiety disorder is no different than the Combat Stress, which leads to Post-Traumatic Stress Disorder. This also explains why I would rather be back in Iraq, because I know where I stand in Iraq during the time of war. But after fighting for my country, it's hard to find my place in America when I see all the racial signs the minute I leave my front door.

How to Respond to Racism

During our Veterans of Color group session, many of us had really good ways to respond to racism. I know I can go on for another fifty pages on how to respond to racism, but I would like to keep it simple. If I had to respond to racism, I would tell the person, "From my experience fighting in Iraq on four separate occasions with my fellow Soldiers, there was no room for racism on the battlefield, so why are you creating racism right here in America?" The bottom line is, can we put the color of our skin, our religious beliefs, and any other differences aside and work together to achieve a common goal? You will hear me say the same thing later in the book.

Wearing the Mask

The purpose of wearing the mask has a lot to do with blacks frequently concealing their pain, frustration, and anger from whites, as well as from one another. The reason for hiding their frustration and anger is because the defeat and desperation have been difficult to articulate, and it can impose deep anxiety on loved ones. If blacks showed true feelings about whites' racial abuse toward blacks, there would have been a great chance of retaliation. From what I've learned about wearing "the mask," in order for a black man or woman to maintain happiness and contentment, they must wear the mask. With that said, it is my opinion that it is truly a bunch of bullshit because we, as service members in the Armed Forces, find it frustrating to see that America is still on this racial bullshit! Let's get it together, people!

How to Make an Impact Against Racism

For starters, I believe my fellow Americans need to get back to basics on understanding the human race. In order to make an impact against racism, we need to understand there is only one race, and that is the human race, which includes Caucasians, Africans, Asians, Indians, Arabs, Latinos, and Jews. This means we all have different ethnicities, but we were all equally created by God.

We, as the human race, need to learn to stop having those special cliques, meaning the Good Old Boys Club. I have noticed in the state of Utah it seems like if you are not part of that inner circle, then you're not accepted. With that said, it seems like the people in Utah are only concerned with their own little private circle: church, friends, kids, jobs, and family. From what I can see, if you're not part of the inner circle, it is hard to be kind and compassionate to one another and forgive each other, just as God forgives us of our sins.

One of the win-win battles against racism in Utah is that I see a majority of the white community involved in the Mormon religion. They are doing a big thing about adopting black African children. Now with that said, I'm wondering if the families are doing this because the upper leaders in the Mormon religion are putting the word out to adopt African children because it's a cool and trendy thing to do. Or is there money in adopting these children? Or are the families adopting the African children out of deep love from their hearts? Either way, it is a good way to expand the minds of people and open their hearts to spread the love for people and end racism. I can see a divided line being drawn straight down the middle. People on one side will have negative views about a white family adopting African children, and people on the other will have positive views about the adoption. Now with white families who have the African children, they will get a taste of how it feels to hear racial remarks. In other words, they will understand how it feels to be a black man or woman who has to deal with racism all day every day. At the same time, the white families with African children can see where the problem starts. They will be able to see it's their own fellow white men and women who continue to add fuel to the racism output in America.

Troubles with Employment after Military Service

Soldiers who have completed their enlistment contract with the military are applauded because they are leaders, dependable, and they work well in teams. Nice, but it doesn't mean much in this competitive job market. It is very hard to make that smooth transition from military to the civilian workforce if military retirees aren't also given the certifications and licenses they earned in the Army to be used when they return to civilian life. I believe that the workforce in America today could give two shits about what one's job was in the military or the true values of getting the job done, not to mention what Army retirees are capable of doing.

So, all of the skills you develop as a Soldier—leadership, being dependable, works well in teams—goes right out the window. I believe the best way for Soldiers to be extremely competitive in the job market is for employers to truly understand what a retiree's job was in the military. The United States Army needs to change how they do business with Soldiers. What I mean is every Soldier who has a job in the United States Army needs to be licensed by the time he or she is promoted to E-5 Sergeant. That rank is equal to a first-line supervisor in the civilian sector. Being licensed should be covered nationwide. So if a Soldier is an E-5 Sergeant and is an electrician, he or she should be a licensed electrician. Same goes for plumbers, carpenters, and heavy equipment operators. When these Soldiers are promoted to the rank of E-6 Staff Sergeant and Sergeant First Class (SFC) E-7, they all should be licensed as contractors.

Besides the Construction Engineer field, other jobs in the Army should be licensed jobs as well, such as Soldiers who are mechanics in the Army. In other words, if you are an E-5 Sergeant Mechanic, you should have an ASE-certified license to be a mechanic in the civilian workforce. When a Soldier gets promoted to E-6 and E-7, he or she should be a licensed master mechanic.

Soldiers who are (88M) truck drivers in the Army should already have their commercial driver's license (CDL) by the time they reach E-5 SGT. They should have some way to keep track of miles they have driven, as well as accident-free mileage. I've seen firsthand with the (88M) drivers traveling all those miles on the road in Iraq, dodging hidden IEDs and RPGs to make sure supplies reach various camps. They don't have a CDL license, yet their lives are on the line every time they are out on the roads. After a Soldier has done multiple tours in Iraq or Afghanistan, delivering supplies, if they decide to end their service in the military and want to become a truck driver and drive on safer roads in the United States, they shouldn't have to go school for six to eight weeks in order to receive their CDL license. That's almost like telling someone to repeat the twelfth grade after having been there and done that.

Another job in the Army that gets the short end of the stick is the combat medic. Combat medics are in the heat of battle being fired upon. They stop a bleeding Soldier's artery from bleeding out, not to mention, stabilize and get him or her to a Medevac chopper. What I'm truly getting at is that these combat medics have saved many lives in the combat zone. After multiple tours in Iraq or Afghanistan, they can't get a job in an emergency room or at a nearby hospital because he or she doesn't have a particular certification or didn't go to this school or that school. So in order for a Soldier to have a smooth transition into the civilian workforce, each Soldier needs to be licensed before they end their service in the military.

My last job description was as a Construction Supervisor (12H) 2010–2013

I performed construction quality assurance/quality control for projects in seventeen facilities within the area of operation (Guam, Saipan, American Samoa, Hawaii, and Alaska.) I was a Non-Commissioned Officer (NCO) who conducted facility repairs/upgrades, provided technical engineering support, and advised on work orders, performed major system repairs and minor construction projects, assisted with coordinating future repairs and facility upgrades, managed accountability of the section's tools, and kept up the tool room and equipment storage facility.

What this job description is saying is that not only can I maintain multiple building repairs in various places, but I can also keep the building repair costs down so that it won't hurt the taxpayer's pockets (versus paying a civilian contractor out of our budget to do the same work that I'm capable of doing.) Even with all of the supervisor skills and various construction trades skills that I've developed in the Army, the only job I can get in the workforce is to buy homes and remodel them to resell or rent them out at an affordable price, which means if I had the money, I would have to buy myself a job. When you buy homes and do that type of work, you're a homeowner, which means you can do what you like in the home as long as it is within the building codes. The funny thing is you don't have to be licensed to remodel your own home just like we Engineer Soldiers weren't licensed to build.

I did all those construction projects all over Iraq, as well as different parts of the world. I was that guy who had to install the ductless A/C units for all of the sea huts we built for our fellow Soldiers and coalition forces. There were about 450 ductless A/C installations that I conducted in 2008 and 2009. None of us were licensed or certified to handle Freon, but when I was in the Army, I had to do what I was told to get it done. Meanwhile, regardless of how much experience I had with the A/C installation, I still can't get a job in the heating and air conditioning field unless I'm a licensed A/C technician, which requires me to go to school for something I already know how to do.

Remodeling homes is the only thing I love to do, and it shows how good my skills are. Home remodeling is the only job that I could have complete control of. I can manage the project from start to finish and teach a few helpers who want to learn about the different aspects of the trade skills, just like I trained my fellow Soldiers in the past. With home remodeling, I still carry the seven Army Core Values (Loyalty, Duty, Respect, Selfless Service, Honor, Integrity, and

Personal Courage). This means my hard work and dedication to the job will show. I've always said (in a joking manner) if I had 2 percent of Oprah's money or 2 percent of Bill Gates' money, I could create a full home remodeling business and create jobs for young adults like Job Corps students and my fellow Soldiers with whom I served as a Construction Engineer. I guess my goal is to be happy with myself at the end of day and create jobs for fellow Vets since our US government won't. Hopefully, my PTSD and nightmares will disappear for good.

Favoritism & Nepotism

Here's an example of why it's so hard for Veterans today to find employment. In the month of February 2014, I e-mailed a supervisor my cover letter and resume with my last job description while enlisted in the United States Army. The job was at a military installation where a civilian company had a contract with the Air Force to perform maintenance on all military housing. I thought my background in construction and home remodeling would be a valuable asset to the company.

Since my last e-mail on February 2014, I noticed that the supervisor hired two new people to work in his department. At the same time, they still had one employee with a bad criminal record who was allowed to work on military housing, which put him in proximity to military spouses and children. The employee was later let go, sometime in March, but ended up being reported in the local newspaper in May 2014 for aggravated assault. He'd held a woman, her husband, and child during a three-hour standoff with local police. What types of background checks are these companies doing to allow someone with a criminal history to work in a military installation around military families? My next question is, why did they hire two new employees who had less experience than me? I have a strong background in construction and home remodeling, not to mention, I'm a retired Veteran with a clean record.

I believe the biggest problem facing Veterans seeking employment is breaking through the inner political games involving favoritism and nepotism. From supervisors to HR managers, nepotism plays a large role. They spend more time hiring their college buddies, golfing buddies, and basically creating the "Good Old Boys Club."

In Hawaii, HR managers and supervisors spent more time hiring their aunts, uncles, nephews, and cousins. The sad thing about hiring friends and relatives is that most of them don't know anything about the job or the position they're holding. Meanwhile, we have Veterans who know how to do the job, but companies won't give us the time of day. Somehow, this game of favoritism nepotism needs to stop.

The Best Way to Create Government Jobs for Veterans

Today's bad economy and government cutbacks leave Soldiers coming home from war jobless after serving their country. There is a way to turn things around and put hardworking Soldiers to work to boost the economy and bring in tax revenue. The best way for these problems to be solved is to create government jobs. One way to create government jobs is to create another Hoover Dam Project.

The Hoover Dam was named after Herbert Hoover, the thirty-first president of the United States. He took office the same year the stock market crashed that led the country into the Great Depression. When Franklin D. Roosevelt was elected president in 1932, he launched a series of economic programs designed to overcome the effects of the Great Depression. One of them was the Hoover Dam. Hoover Dam was the largest building project the federal government had undertaken during the 1930s. More than two hundred engineers worked to design the dam that would be constructed in the Black Canyon. The concrete arch gravity structure was intended to prevent flooding, as well as provide much-needed irrigation and hydroelectric power to states like California and Arizona.

By the time the project began, thousands of prospective workers had rushed to the region, many of which had lost their jobs during the first years of the Great Depression. A total of twenty-one thousand men worked on building the dam over the course of its construction. The Hoover Dam Project occupied five thousand men at any given time. The region's growing population turned Las Vegas from a sleepy town into a bustling city. The nearby town of Boulder City was created specifically to house and feed the workers who built the dam, not to mention the manufacturers who manufactured parts for the project site, like the penstock pipe. Penstock pipes were used as a cooling system through which water ran. The pipes were embedded into concrete in order for the concrete to curve evenly and not dry out too fast due to the heat. Over 580 miles of cooling pipes were embedded in 4.5 million cubic yards of concrete, and the concrete dam is still curving after seventy-five years.

My observation is this: the Hoover Dam Project got people back to work during the Great Depression. It took twenty-one thousand men to make this project happen. Every job on that site was important. If you were a fuel handler, you made sure running equipment was full of fuel, which meant you had a job for the next five years, and from each paycheck you paid your federal taxes. Hoover Dam not only created jobs for men on the job site but also created jobs for outside businesses, like gas stations for fuel and oil. Food, water, transportation, clothing stores, restaurants, and hospitals became valuable and crucial outside resources that required extra manpower to support the Hoover Dam Project. The outside resources brought in more tax revenue that was being drawn in for the government to create funded programs other than welfare.

So my question is this: Can our government strategize another project similar to the Hoover Dam Project to get the American people and our fellow Soldiers back to work and strengthen our economy? If so, let's create a desalination plant somewhere in Southern California. Our government can create a desalination project by pumping ocean water into the desalination plant to turn it into fresh water so that our farmers in California can beat the drought and grow their crops to feed America. After all, we all need to put fresh fruits and vegetables on the table for our family. So Congress, stop shining the seats with your asses, let's figure how many resources are involved to make this project happen, and let's put Veterans to work so we can translate our skills and leadership into today's workforce.

Keeping Your Trade Skills in Shape

Despite the job opportunities to share my leadership skills and various construction trade skills I learned as a Construction Engineer in the United States Army, I spent my weekends helping my brother and his girlfriend with a major plumbing problems in their home. As a retired Staff Sergeant, I believe in order to maintain those high-level skill sets you've gained while serving your country, you have to sharpen your skills by volunteering your skill sets to others who need your help. I think it is no different than a person spending some time working out at the gym to maintain their perfect body shape. We all know we can't sit on our asses on the couch expecting to maintain a perfect body shape. Well, I can't sit on my ass, expecting my construction skill sets to be in tip-top shape.

One Friday afternoon, my brother and I were trying to troubleshoot the low water pressure on an old house he and his girlfriend had bought in Ogden, Utah. The house was built in the 1960s. With a house that old, you're looking at an uphill battle on solving the low water pressure. When we got under the house, I knew things were going to be pretty tight for me because I'm a big guy. But there was about three feet of extra space because the earth dipped down far enough to where I could sit down upright and see how the plumbing was routed out, using flashlights and other lighting gadgets. While my brother and I sat by the water shutoff valve, I noticed the major problem that they were having with the lower water pressure issue. The pipes coming into the house were three-quarter-inch galvanized pipes, but shortly after the water shutoff valve, the pipes were reduced to half-inch copper pipes that ran through the house. That explained the low water pressure.

If they were in the shower on the third floor, and someone was washing dishes on the second floor, then they would lose water pressure in the shower as well as in other areas because of the low volume of water traveling to the water outlets. After my assessment, I came up with a plan to take out most of the half-inch copper pipes and replace them with three-quarter-inch copper pipes, starting after the water shutoff valve. My brother and I ran about seventy feet of three-quarter-inch cooper pipes. It wasn't an easy task to be under the house for twenty-two hours, soldering copper fittings to copper pipes. Since my brother was much smaller than I was, he was able to connect the pipes together with my proper guidance. When all of the pipes were connected, we were able to turn the water on and check for leaks to see if the water pressure had improved.

I'm happy to say, "Mission accomplished." My brother was happy and so was his girlfriend. I realized that my skill set and my supervisor skills were still in top shape, and my plumbing theory was correct when it came to water volume and pressure. In the beginning, I had to give my brother a crash course on how plumbing systems worked. Since I was unemployed, I did volunteer work in order to keep my skill sets in shape for future employment.

Volunteer Work in Jamestown, Colorado

Jamestown was an old mining town back in 1883, sitting at an elevation of 6,920 feet above sea level. Three hundred Americans lived in Jamestown, but only 20 percent have moved back to Jamestown after the massive flood in September 2013.

On 25 April 2014, I drove from Syracuse, Utah, to Jamestown, Colorado, (541 miles) to team up with a nonprofit. The organization consisted of mostly all combat Vets who served in Iraq and Afghanistan more than once. Members from the four branches of the military joined together in a two-day event to pull out eighty-foot trees that slid down the mountains into the Jamestown Creek. These could have caused a blockage, which would create another flood in the upper part of Jamestown.

On Saturday and Sunday, we carpooled up the road as far as it went. Then we hiked up half a mile on the side of the mountain with our cutting gear and other equipment. We went along the side of the mountain and up toward the creek where the trees were creating a blockage. Using nothing but chain saws and ropes, we pulled trees out of the creek to be cut down to manageable logs. It required strong arms, legs, and shoulders to manually haul the three-foot by fifteen-inch logs on our shoulders. We then walked, carrying them through rough terrain to a staging area so they could be hauled away properly. With team cohesion, dedication, and the military motto that's embedded in our DNA ("Get 'er done"), the mission was accomplished.

I have to say, working with fellow combat Vets made me feel like I was part of a team. There's nothing like working with over forty Veterans getting things done in a time of need. I truly missed the camaraderie after retiring on November 22, 2013, from Schofield Barracks in Hawaii.

As I drove through the mountain roads heading to Jamestown for the first time, I saw how badly the roads were washed away by the massive flood in September 2013. I learned later that the roads were inaccessible for a few months, and most of the citizens of Jamestown temporarily lived elsewhere. Since roads were inaccessible during the disastrous flood, the National Guard stepped in with the Mandatory Evacuation Order. They provided Black Hawks and Chinook helicopters to start evacuating the people from Jamestown to safety into Boulder, Colorado. Somehow, I think the town itself didn't receive federal aid from the US government, but federal aid was provided to individuals and families to build homes for their families.

The thing that bothers me about our government is without federal aid to the town itself, how can Jamestown get back on its feet if they can't rebuild the infrastructure of the town? Major repairs were still needed to keep the old mining town functioning, like the restoration of the water supply to the town and homes, as well as a sewage system, power, and communication. The town could not function without repairs to their infrastructure. Jamestown only received support from various nonprofit organizations. Every little bit helped when it came to getting the town back on its feet. I would like to thank all of the nonprofit organizations that took time to give support to the people in Jamestown. May God bless you all. I can't wait for the next mission so I can reunite with fellow Veterans and "Get 'er done."

The two-day mission at Jamestown was well worth the effort for me to drive a thousand miles round trip and sleep in my truck for two days in order to be part of a team of Veterans helping the Jamestown people get their life back in order. If I were the guy who won the Mega Millions lottery, I would dedicate my time and energy to help rebuild, and I would stay there until every last resident of Jamestown could come home.

Adjusting to Retirement Life

On the day I retired, it seemed like all text messages about meetings, formation, briefings, or offers to work on projects just stopped. I kind of understood what a child movie star back in the early eighties went through when they were no longer a popular kid as they got older. They had outgrown the child roles, and there were no adult roles for them because they were always known as the "child" movie star. Just like I was always known as Sergeant Duckworth who knew his job as a Construction Engineer, so now I was just another face out in the civilian sector.

I didn't know what else to do with my time. Instead of being happy that I retired from the Army I felt confused and out of place. The only thing worse than being retired and coming back from Iraq or Afghanistan was trying to live here among the simple-minded Americans who didn't think outside the box to solve problems or show team cohesion. It is hard to be around people who are not mission driven or goal oriented. In other words, in the military, everything is structured. You engage in a mission and you get things done without the drama. This is the part where I wish I was still back in Iraq, because I had a sense of purpose and I enjoyed being a part of a fast-paced organization that had the common goal of completing the mission.

A retired Veteran and an unemployed citizen look a lot like twins when they have nothing but time on their hands. I tried to make the most of my time while still living in Hawaii. I did the one thing I said I would do if I was retired and that was to get up early and just watch people the same age as me go to work and deal with the battle of traffic. Meanwhile, I traveled ten minutes down the hill from Makakilo to Ko Olina to have breakfast on the beach and look at the ocean. Later, I would go to the movies around noon and, at times, I found myself being the only person in the movie theater. I could watch the movie in peace versus having to wonder if there would be another shooting in the movie theater like in Colorado. After the movies, I would have ice cream and be right back in Ko Olina close by the ocean. At times, I was there way after sundown because I never wanted to go home. Going home to an empty house was more depressing, but at the same time it was my only protection against being out in public. If I was having a bad day, my empty house was my safe haven. I would not answer my door either if I didn't have an idea of who was there. Besides being home alone, when I went to places like Ko Olina I tried to make my day as easy as Sunday morning and be peaceful and happy.

Before retirement, I had a vision of someone with a flexible work schedule being with me in public, helping me enjoy being out in public, or doing activities a little differently in public. I met a new friend while doing side jobs working on wall repairs in Hawaii Kai. She did house cleaning part time, and she did volunteer work on educating people about hepatitis B and C through a nonprofit origination in Honolulu. I noticed right off the bat that we both had the same interests and one of them was helping others. I believed that was the beginning of having a trustworthy friendship, and she saw how much care I put into my work and made sure that my customers were happy with my work.

During our spare time, which was mostly every day for me, I would call her up to have dinner with me since I didn't cook for myself. The purpose of my newfound friendship was for dinner companionship, to help me to be out in public more, and to help me enjoy life a little. I wanted to laugh and talk and not have to be alone and look at everyone as a potential threat. At restaurants, she would help me take my focus off of everyone and focus on her and our conversation. I wish all restaurants would stop having their employees sing "Happy Birthday" and clap their hands. It is hard enough for Veterans to be out in public, and loud noises startle Veterans dealing with PTSD. It immediately puts us on edge and truly disrupts our dinner and conversations. To all the birthday people who like to go to restaurants for their birthdays, I would like for you to shut the hell up and stop looking for attention. Have your birthday dinner in peace so that Veterans with PTSD can have their dinner in peace. Just think, people, how many Soldiers have spent their birthdays in Iraq or Afghanistan? Do you think the war stopped because it was a Soldier's birthday? No it didn't, so again shut the hell up, enjoy your birthday dinner in peace, and don't have a waiter or waitress come to your table to sing to you "Happy Birthday." After dinner, my friend and I would head to Ko Olina to watch the sunset by the ocean, which was one of my favorite peaceful pastimes.

Most of my dinnertimes weren't like most people who would have dinner around six or seven o'clock. Mine was early, around 4:30, so I could be in the restaurant with fewer people and avoid the "Happy Birthday" bull crap. When my good friend helped me change my ways about being in public, I found I was less hypervigilant. When it came to hanging out in sports bars, we didn't go on a Friday or Saturday night. Instead, we went on Tuesday nights in downtown Waikiki. It was a nice experience.

I was really grateful that I met her because without her, I believe I wouldn't hang out like she had me do. It was also like she knew what a Veteran with PTSD needed. I found out she had a friend at Schofield Barracks who was a Senior Non-Commission Officer (NCO) who spent multiple tours in Afghanistan as a combat medic. Throughout our time together, the NCO shared some stories of what Soldiers go through during wartime situations and the side effects that Soldiers endure when they come home. So between the NCO stories and stories of my struggles with overcoming issues with PTSD, it seemed like she knew what to do to help me get back on my feet. My circle of friends was very small due to me having a lack of trust in civilian people, but she is part of my circle of friends right along with my three high-school buddies and my fellow Soldiers.

I remember two occasions when my good friend saw the war side of me, but it was only for her protection. We were at Kmart getting a few items and I decided to use the ATM while she shopped for a few items. As I was at the ATM getting cash, there was this weird guy looking and smiling while I withdrew my cash. The funny thing was he was one arm's length away from me just smiling. My first thought was to knock his head off for being too close to me at the ATM, but I would go to jail for hitting a person. But it was okay for this dumb ass to be very close to me at the ATM machine. Since my inner rage and hypervigilance kicked in, it had me thinking that everyone in the store was a potential threat. I began to look for my friend. Luckily she was at the cash register paying for her items. I noticed a guy behind her just looking straight down on her, not the look like he was checking her out. As I approached the register to check to see if she had everything she needed, I was still looking at the guy behind her, wondering what the hell he was looking down at her for. When my friend paid for her items, the guy stopped her and tried to give a sad story about having trouble cashing a check. I stopped him mid-sentence and said, "Look, man, we don't have time for your bullshit!" I told my friend, "Let's go and let's go now!" When we got outside the store, she asked me what was wrong with me. I guess she saw the look in my eyes that I wasn't playing around about getting out of the store because of the guy. I told her that the guy was trying to pull a fast one on her about some damn check he couldn't cash. I told her I was watching him from a distance, and I could tell he was up to something. She looked in her purse and realized that she had left one of her pockets open inside her purse, and she had a few $100 bills, $50 bills, and some $20 bills. So I told her that explained why he was looking down on her so hard. If I didn't show up to the register to wait on her, he would have tried to rob her, but he had to play it off by making a sad story about a check he couldn't cash. So basically I just prevented a robbery by being hypervigilant, but it was that weird guy smiling at me at the ATM that triggered my hypervigilance and inner rage that made me want to knock someone's head off.

The second occasion was when she was on H1 heading home around ten o'clock in the evening, and I was driving home from a side job on the same highway. I got off my exit to Makakilo Drive and my friend called me to tell me that someone had been following her for about twelve miles. I asked her how she knew she was being followed, and she said she had been switching lanes and doing ten miles over the speed limit.

I told her, "Whatever you do, don't go straight home." By this time I'd already made it home and parked in the parking stall at my condo. She mentioned that she just passed Ko Olina, so I told her to drive to McDonald's in Waianae because it was well lit. As she was talking to me on the phone, she did not know I was on my way to meet her in the McDonald's parking lot to find out who was following her. When I arrived at the parked lot, I parked at a safe distance, but I could get a clear view of my friend's car as I scanned the parking lot to see who had been following her. When I saw someone approach her car, I started to approach her car as well. When I got to her car, it turns out it was one if her relatives who had been following her, but her cousin had bought a new car so that was why my friend didn't recognize the car that was following her. She told her cousin that she was scared as hell and didn't want go home. At the same time, my friend was surprised that I even came down to make sure she was safe. I told her once before that, as a combat Veteran, whoever is with me is like family; I will always protect them with my life, and I will always make sure that nothing bad happens to them as long as I'm around. I guess she didn't believe it then, but after I showed up at the McDonald's parking lot, she knew I was not playing when it came to protecting the people around me. She said that even though I was fighting the battles of PTSD, she still felt safe with me.

Adjusting to Home in Utah

I was welcomed home, but I felt so out of place because my wife and daughter had a life, a routine, and schedule of their own. I was like a fish out of water. I even lost the drive to plan a retirement party because looking at everyone's busy life schedule made it seem like they were happy that I was retired but at the same time they could care less. At least that's the vibe I felt when I dealt with people. I spent about eighteen months away from my family while dealing with my treatment and looking after my retirement benefits, so I wasn't with my wife when she got us a home to live in nor did I see my daughter enrolled in school.

For the first sixty days or so in Utah, I just stayed out of the way. Not only had I stayed out of the way, I even slept downstairs in the basement in the extra bedroom. There wasn't much in it; it was just like the sleeping quarters I was in at Camp Marez in Mosul, Iraq. I darkened the room by putting a blanket over the window. I had a box spring and mattress on the floor and the mink blanket I had from Iraq. The sad thing was that was all I needed. It's interesting that many children are afraid of being in the dark, but for me, being in a dark room is the safest place. I was not in the master bedroom with my wife because I would go to bed at three in the morning, and she needed her sleep because she had to get up and work. I just did not want to disturb her sleeping. At the same time, I'd spent so long not sleeping in the bed with my wife that I had just gotten too comfortable sleeping alone. As I mentioned earlier, I had spent about eighteen months away from her dealing with my issues with PTSD. I believe I truly lost that connection of being a husband; I treat my wife as a best friend. We were like perfect roommates, but I stayed downstairs in the basement.

My wife's everyday life consisted of going to the gym, which she had never done before leaving Hawaii. I was happy for her that she was looking after her health, but when I looked at her, in the back in my mind, I thought, *Who is this woman? Where is my wife?* When I hugged her, it was almost like I was hugging someone else. Her routine was so far ahead of mine that it was almost like I was not needed in the house. On Saturdays, she would go and help prep the church for Sunday and Wednesday service, and on Thursday, there was Bible study. Not to mention, she worked Monday through Friday. Meanwhile, I was trying to get my life up and running, but it was going at a snail's pace. I love my wife and the fact that she has stuck by me through eighteen years, most of which were spent with me in the military. Shortly after we were stationed at Fort Sill, Oklahoma, 9/11 happened and in 2003 I did my first tour in Iraq. During the six years of my tours, running back and forth to Iraq, our marriage was put to the test regarding how long we could hold on to it.

I believe after the second tour to Iraq, I ended up coming back as a different person. Even though my wife stayed with me through the toughest times, I felt like such a failure after 2010. I just wanted to end my marriage because I thought her life would be much better than dealing with a Soldier with PTSD and still struggling to adjust to civilian life. I believed life was too short, and my wife gave up a lot of things to be with someone who served and fought for his country. I felt that I put so many burdens on my wife and that it was best for her not to be with me. I thought her life would be much better with someone else, someone not struggling with PTSD.

We had two properties, and I lost both of them when I got out of active duty in 2010. At that time, I was running away from my PTSD issues, and it didn't help that I couldn't find a job to maintain both properties. The sad thing was that I had my family one step away from being homeless because I couldn't find work. I always ask myself, *If I am separated from my wife, will I be able to love again?* Maybe not. The average person has no clue how to understand the struggles of being normal in civilian life while still struggling with

PTSD. I believe I would be much happier if I lived alone and enjoyed life at my own pace, but I would still be best friends with my wife.

Road Trips Are Another Form of Therapy

My first road trip happened in April 2014 when I had to fly down to Oakland to pick up my truck that arrived at the Richmond port after traveling from Honolulu. I remember my wife asked me when I would return home. At first, I told her three days because I felt like I needed to be back as soon as possible, as if I had a job to come back to. But I realized that I was retired and could come home when I was ready. After I got my truck back in my possession, I stayed in the Bay Area for about eight days before I decided to head back to Utah. I stayed eight days to find out if my theory was right about how to reset my mind maybe overcome the issues of war. I figured in order to move forward with my life, I had to find the things that made me happy. The best way to bring out my happiness was to go far back into my childhood and get rid of the battle mind-set. I had to go back home and walk the streets that I grew up in. I'm talking about walking and breathing the fresh air, walking on the Berkeley Pier where my daddy used to take us fishing and breathe in the ocean breeze, and looking toward the Golden Gate Bridge and the new Bay Bridge. I went to Curtis Street where we had fifteen kids on the block who all got along. That was the same street that my dad would have the grill going on in the backyard, and the whole neighborhood smelled like barbecue. On Friday nights, there would be a fish fry night when my dad and our close friends would come over and have some fish and play spades or dominos while listening to their favorite songs from The Temptations, The O Jays, and Earth, Wind & Fire. Outside of the Bay, I walked the grounds of my high school at Fairfield High and visited my second family, the Jenkins family. I looked at the building that used to be Church's Fried Chicken where I worked during high school. I believed that being around things that made me happy from back in the day might help me reset my mind back to what it was before the war began. I had to overcome this battle mind-set and the PTSD. People do not understand that when you do four tours to Iraq or Afghanistan, you lose what's normal. Today, I still struggle with what is normal. How does it feel to laugh? Or play? Or go on a family vacation?

During my eight-day stay in the Bay, I even paid a visit to the old Boys Club I used to attend when I was about twelve or thirteen years old. The Boys Club was in west Oakland, off of 24th and Market Street. When I was a little boy, my dad thought The Boys Club would be a good place for my brother and me to hang out, because living in the city of Oakland made it easy for young boys to get caught up in street gangs or the drug scene. Between the fear of the old school ass whooping and the structured program that The Boys Club had, it kept my brother and me out of trouble and out of the life that the streets of Oakland had to offer at that time.

As I walked through The Boys Club, watching all the young kids doing homework and having reading time, it really transported me back in time when I was a little boy doing the same thing. As I sat down and looked at all the positive things I had seen going on, I had to sit there and smile. As I was smiling, a little voice in the back of my head told me that this was the reason I fought for this country. I fought to protect these kids' futures and for the first time, I got it.

Once I understood why I fought for this country, I would fight again in Iraq or any other place to protect these young kids' futures. After seeing positive things going on at The Boys Club, I could see that after all these years, the same club that I attended as a little boy was still providing a safe haven for young boys and girls and helping them further their education by providing a fun learning environment. I just wish there were more Boys and Girls Clubs in the Bay Area so more kids had a safe place to go to after school, instead of running the streets and getting into trouble. I wish I lived in Oakland and worked for The Boys Club. I wouldn't care how much money I made, but what I would care about was me giving back to The Boys Club, which kept me out of the streets. I would mentor the kids and teach them how important education is. I believe working for The

Boys Club would give me a sense of purpose to start my days, by mentoring kids and watching them grow.

After my visit to The Boys Club, I drove to East Oakland. I don't know why I drove there, but I guess my truck just took me there. As I was driving through some of the old neighborhoods I used to know, I realized for the first time I felt like a Soldier in the battlefield without my weapon. Meaning my PTSD caused me to be in that Iraq mode and super hypervigilant.

With all the violence in the hood, I needed my M4 for protection. I stopped at Church's Fried Chicken on 73rd and Bancroft to have lunch. It had been years since I had fried okra and Cajun rice. Having lunch there took me back to memories of working in Church's Fried Chicken in Fairfield during my high-school days. In fact, I still remember the names and faces of the people with whom I worked.

My memories were cut short because I noticed trouble about to happen when the young thugs came into the restaurant bad-mouthing the employees and trying to start trouble. I looked at my truck outside and I noticed that I had parked my truck in backwards so when it was time to go, it was easy to drive forward and keep moving. I also noticed the way I parked the truck allowed me an easy exit out of the parking lot, which told me I still had that war habit of backing our vehicles up so that we could easily exit out of a kill zone. As these young thugs kept acting a fool, I cut my lunch short and left as quickly as I could. I wasn't for sure if the knuckleheads who had their pants sagging way past their asses had weapons. Since I felt so defenseless, I just left and took that exit out of the parking lot. As I was leaving, the whole time I wished I had my M4 with a loaded thirty-round magazine. As I mentioned before, I felt like a Soldier who didn't have his weapon in the battlefield. Shit, I looked at East Oakland and West Oakland as being one big battlefield.

I headed up to 73rd Street to jump on Freeway 580 toward Fairfield to see my second family. I had arrived just in time to watch the local news. From what I saw, a thirty-year-old woman shot a sixteen-year-old boy as he was walking home from school. It all started as an altercation that ended up a physical fight, then the woman shot her gun. Come to find out the woman had an issue with a family member of the sixteen-year-old boy's but took the problem out on the young boy by taking his life. I was so upset and tense that my head hurt. I believe from riding the streets of Oakland and seeing those young thugs acting a fool and listening to the news, I realized I couldn't put my battle skills behind me—my war-fighting capabilities (like shoot to kill) and my issues with PTSD. If I lived in Oakland, I would always be on guard and ready to kill. I believed that my battle skills would be so keyed up to where I would have to buy the civilian version of the M4 and all the ammo I could carry and have it with me at all times, as if I had never left Iraq.

For the first time—even though I'm not a big fan of the state of Utah—I was happy that I lived in a town (Syracuse) that was drama free. During this road trip, I learned how one type of living environment (living in Oakland) may cause me to stay in that battle mind-set, which causes me to be more hypervigilant, looking for something bad to happen so that I can react to the danger and constantly be on edge. My behavior would show that I never left Iraq or Afghanistan. On the other hand, living in a midsize country town, like Syracuse, Utah, my battle mind-set and hypervigilance dropped drastically. Now that doesn't mean I let my guard down completely; it just means that my guard is not as high as if I lived in Oakland.

My visit with the Jenkins family was cut short, but I promised them that the next visit would be longer. I was excited to put my 2004 Dodge Hemi on the road for the road trip to Utah and see for the first time if my engine really had the power of a hemi. Since I bought the truck in Honolulu, it was kind of hard to see what the hemi could do out on the roads there because I was constantly stuck in stop-and-go traffic. Everyone on that island knows that the H1 freeway is a hot mess.

As I began my travel on Highway 80, heading east to Syracuse from Fairfield, California, I felt a sense of freedom and open space as I drove my big, white Dodge Hemi with the flow master making that powerful exhaust sound. The sense of freedom must have come from being stuck on the island of Honolulu for ten years, but the feeling was bigger than that. After a while on the road, I was thinking about what the Vietnam and Korean War Veterans did when they ended their service in the military and found the sense of freedom on the open roads of America. I don't know when Route 66 was created, but I believed a lot of service members back then bought brand-new motorcycles they been waiting to get after the war and jumped on Route 66 to ride until the wheels fell off, enjoying the sense of freedom and breathing the fresh air, versus breathing the smell of war and death.

As I drove over Donner Pass through the Sierra Mountains of California, I admired how much power the old hemi had. After all, my truck had been stuck on the island. I came down a hill and saw this nice pretty blue lake. My first thought was, *I bet there's some good fishing,* but my thought was disrupted because I saw an unidentified vehicle on the side of the road. Vehicles like that, on the side of the roads in Iraq, meant bad business—parked vehicles may be loaded with IEDs. Highway 80 in this area is a two-lane road, so I was in the left lane trying to get past this unidentified vehicle. As I passed the parked vehicle, I saw markings on the driver's side door that read CHP (California Highway Patrol). My first thought was, *Why do they want to be under cover and blend in as if they're just like any other normal vehicle?*

At that moment, I was put into defense mode to the point of not trusting the undercover highway patrol car. I didn't trust that cop car any more than I trusted the Iraqi police. The police officer finally pulled me over three miles later. He said that he clocked me on the radar coming down the hill at seventy-eight miles per hour and when I passed him, he clocked me at eighty-three. I told him I was a retired Soldier and by seeing an unidentified vehicle on the side of the road, I felt like I was entering a kill zone.

He asked me how many tours I did in Iraq and I told him four. I also told him that from January 2003 to November 2009 I spent six years running back and forth to Iraq, conducting road repair missions and other construction missions. After my vehicle paperwork checked out clean, along with shipping papers from the port, my story made sense and the officer let me go without giving me a ticket.

When I arrived in Reno, Nevada, I stopped to get fuel. I wasn't on empty at all; in fact, I was only at three-quarters of a tank. I figured if I filled up now, I could make it to Elko, Nevada, which would put me at a half a tank after driving 260 miles from Reno. After filling up in Elko, the full tank of gas should take me all the way to my driveway in Syracuse, Utah. The purpose of planning my fuel stops was to avoid unnecessary stops. I guess I was constantly on my convoy mind-set as if I was still in Iraq. Hell, do you think we would get on the radio to request a fuel stop or a bathroom break while driving on the roads in Iraq? No, we didn't. In fact, during our convoy most of us Soldiers became very talented in pissing in makeshift piss bottles while the convoys was hauling ass.

As I drove on Highway 80 East heading toward my next fuel stop in Elko, Nevada, I had a memory of the countless road repair missions I was involved in after an IED exploded in Iraq. I started to wonder how tragic it would be if parts of Highway 80 were destroyed due to IEDs going off, disrupting the flow of travel. Throughout the stretch of highway, at speeds of eighty miles an hour, I think I counted anywhere from seventy-five to one hundred possible spots where IEDs could be planted. The places I saw for potential IEDs were concrete tunnels that ran across but under the highway. These spots were deadly in Iraq. The insurgents would plant thousands of pounds of IEDs. As Engineer Soldiers, I still remember how we slowed down the insurgents from destroying the roads. Let's just say, if IEDs ever occurred on our highways, I knew just the materials that would put a stop to IEDs exploding inside the concrete tunnels that were used for water runoff under the highways, and at the same time keeping Veterans like me gainfully employed.

When I arrived at my next fuel stop in Elko, Nevada, my brother texted me and asked my location. I thought it was odd he was asking me about my location, but later he texted me random lines or quotes from the 1970s car movie *Smokey and the Bandit*. My brother brought back some good humor by sending me quotes from the movie like, "Snowman, do you got your ears on? What's your twenty? Where are you?" Or he would send me quotes from the character, Sheriff Buford T. Justice from Texas saying, "I'm Smokey Bear and I'm tail grabbing your ass right now." As you can see, still to this day, *Smokey and the Bandit* is our favorite movie of all time. In fact, I still remember the country song that plays at the beginning of the movie. Now, that doesn't mean I love country music it just means I like that song.

After I filled up in Elko and jumped back on the road, my brother still texted me random quotes from the movie and had me laughing to myself. I could picture the movie scene in my head as I was driving. At times I was in deep thought about our favorite movie. I guess it was a good thing. It kept my mind away from being in that convoy mind-set like I had been before my fuel stop. The part that kept me in somewhat of a convoy mind-set was that I knew I had to keep the big hemi moving. Thank goodness that the speed limit was eighty miles per hour, though at times I was five or ten miles over the speed limit. I kept moving toward my final destination. There had been times when I was on a convoy in Iraq and we missed an IED explosion by a few seconds or by a few minutes due to the speed we were traveling. So that truly explains why when I'm on the roads, I like to keep it moving with fewer bathroom breaks.

When I finally made it home to Syracuse, I had to say to myself, *Mission accomplished.* The big hemi did extremely well on the roads. I like the fact the it had so much power while climbing the mountains through Donner Pass and other places. The newer trucks of today were getting out of the hemi's way while climbing through those mountains. The funny thing is my truck is ten years older than some of those newer trucks and with one hundred sixty-five thousand miles on it. I guess they don't make trucks like they used to.

The Second Road Trip

My second road trip occurred during the Fourth of July weekend while heading up to Lewiston and Sand Point, Idaho, with my wife, daughter, and mother-in-law. The Idaho trip was our first family trip in years. Prior to this trip, I had thoughts about getting on Highway 15 and driving north. These thoughts happened almost every night around eleven. It makes me feel like I have somewhere to be, like another convoy mission as if I'm still in Mosul. At times, I would feel more wide awake and alert, and I believed that was why I always felt like I had somewhere to be. With this road trip heading north, I was hoping it would help me get rid of this urge to get up and drive north after eleven.

Two days prior to the trip, I did some maintenance on the big hemi as if I was on a road mission to Baghdad. I checked all my tires, lights, and all fluids. I even did an oil change and topped the truck off with fuel. At this point, the truck was ready for the road trip up north. The truck sat for two days before we rolled out. I loaded up the ice chest with ice and drinks and loaded up our luggage in the back of truck. On the day of the trip, we didn't leave until the late evening when my wife got off of work. The road trip started off a little rocky since I discovered my left signal wasn't working. I was upset because I did all my maintenance checks two days prior. After about forty-five minutes at the auto store, I purchased a new lightbulb then we were on our way to Idaho.

While on the road, the weather was rainy and high winds blew across the highway, but the old hemi kept pushing on. My convoy mind-set was on. Our first fill-up was in Boise, Idaho, 319 miles from home, so we decided to also have dinner at the local restaurant. Somehow the weather cleared up but the sun was setting when we left Boise, and we were no longer on the interstate. Instead, we ended up on the two-lane country backroads. Most of the two-lane country roads reminded me of the roads we traveled as we convoyed out of downtown Mosul in 2008 and 2009. Most of the time, as I drove with my family, I forgot where we were driving and forgot that this trip was supposed to be a family road trip. Basically, I was in deep thought about the convoy missions in Iraq, remembering the radio conversations and who was all on the missions.

As we traveled into the late night in unknown territory, I mentioned to my wife that if we ever drove through here again, we needed to leave our house at two in the morning. That way as we drove through the mountain roads, it would be daylight and we could see the roads. Driving through the mountain roads caused my hypervigilance to kick in, leaving a ringing noise in my left ear. I was in the battle mind-set driving through the darkness. None of my coping skills from the PTSD group session were working. All I knew was that my cell phone was fully charged and my truck was still moving, but that soon was disrupted and my combat mind-set was put on full alert. The battery gauge on my truck shot down to zero; its normal reading is in the middle of the gauge.

I kept driving because my headlights weren't dimming out and the truck ran strong. I remember passing a gas station but I kept pushing forward, hoping I could get to the next town. I drove through one more set of uphill mountains roads and as I came out of the mountains and onto another two-lane country road, electrical issues started with the truck. By this time, it was around 11:30 at night, the headlights started flickering, and all power was almost lost from the truck.

I saw a farmhouse with a bright flood light over the front door so I figured I had just enough power to coast into their driveway and find some help. As I approached the long, dirt road driveway, I saw that the gate was locked. I had lost all power along with the power steering and I had to slam on the brakes before I crashed into the wooden gate. The big hemi was like a battleship, dead in the water with no power. I figured it had to be the battery that died, but I remember I had replaced the battery a year prior. The three adults with cell phones in the truck tried to call out by dialing 911 but we kept losing signal, though at least our cell phones where fully charged. We sat in the driveway for ten to fifteen minutes after we lost signal of communication. I first decided I would walk back to the last gas station for some help, but then again I didn't want to leave my family out on the road without protection. If I had a gun in the truck, it would be okay.

Eventually, I started up the truck and it started up like nothing wrong with it. I immediately backed out onto the road and burned rubber heading back to the last gas station we saw. I believed I was about six or eight miles out from the last gas station, but I had to drive back through the mountain roads. As we came out of the mountain roads, I saw the lights of the gas station, and my truck went completely dead. But at least we were about three to four miles out from the gas station that was lit up. Since we were close to the gas station, the signal on our cell phones worked, and we were able to get a tow truck out to assist us with my truck problem.

As we waited, a vehicle stopped a few yards ahead. It looked like they wanted to help us, but somehow they had a second thought and left. Now being in distress, I was happy that they left because my first thought was, *Are they willing to help me while my family is stuck on the road? Or are they here to rob me or to try to kill us?* My combat mind-set was on high alert, and trusting people I didn't know was unlikely. So I was glad the unknown vehicle chose to leave without helping us.

The tow truck finally showed up. The driver looked at the situation and I mentioned to him that the alternator went out on us. He asked how I knew that, and I told him that I lost all electrical power. Then he asked me what if it was just the battery? I told him that I would need both parts replaced so I could continue with my travels. Then he told me that because the next day was the Fourth of July, the parts store would be closed and the auto shop would be closed too. I got the feeling he was adding more problems to a problem that already existed, and I found every bit of energy not to lose control of my anger and frustration and put my negative energy toward the tow trucker. I finally told him, "Look, man, give me a solution so I can get my truck back on the road by morning."

The best solution he gave was that he could take two passengers to a hotel in Cascade, Idaho. I asked him how far it was. He pointed down the road where we saw the lights on at the gas station. He also mentioned that the four-star hotel was right across the street from the gas station. It was hard for me to believe him because we drove on that same road and didn't see a four-star hotel. I don't know if I had tunnel vision, but the only landmark I was concerned with was the gas station. I know it was dark around 11:30 p.m., but I didn't see any four-star hotel off the side of the road. But then again, when driving through a town like Cascade, Idaho, if you blink your eyes more than twice you will drive right out of the mom-and-pop town and not even know that you drove through a small town.

When the tow truck arrived at the hotel with my truck and my family, it turned out to be a nice four-star hotel with great hospitality. The staff members welcomed us with open arms and understood our car troubles. They said that the checkout time was at noon, but we were more than welcome to stay on the property and use the indoor pool until we got our truck up and running. We even had a complimentary breakfast. By the time we paid for our rooms and got settled in and ready for bed, it was 1:30 in the morning. My best solution was to call my brother in Ogden, Utah, to give him a heads up on the car trouble and have him purchase a new alternator and a battery for the truck. I didn't want to call him because he had neck surgery that same week and had to drive four hundred miles to deliver the alternator and battery. After calling my brother, he agreed to make the trip to meet with me with the parts I needed, along with his mechanic tools to do the job. The only drawback was he had to wait until the parts store opened around seven or eight in the morning on Independence Day.

About five hours later, he and his girlfriend arrived with the parts and tools. I could tell that my brother was in bad shape trying to recover from his neck surgery. I felt so bad for bothering him with my car trouble, but at that point, I had no choice but to ask for his help. I don't know of any brothers will go that far to help their brother in need, but I know my brother did that for me. That put my brother in the same category as my fellow brothers and sisters with whom I served in Iraq. In other words, you help your fellow service members in combat as well as back home. We, as fellow Veterans, will stop what we're doing to help our fellow service members, and that was what my brother did for me.

With my brother's guidance, I replaced the bad alternator and battery. It only took me about forty-five minutes to replace everything and have the truck up and running. I thanked my brother very much for making the four hundred-mile trip and gave him seven hundred dollars for his troubles and to cover the cost for the battery and alternator. I gathered up the family from the pool area and thanked the hotel manager for their great hospitality. You know it's funny how you can get the greatest customer service from a small mom-and-pop business rather than a corporate company.

After getting the family back in the truck and continuing on with our road trip, I decided to get gas from that gas station I saw during the night. We had 198 miles to go before we arrived in Lewiston, Idaho. I really didn't need gas, but I still ended up across the street at the gas station. As I got out of the truck, I noticed a young man with a girlfriend or wife and their baby in the car, but he was standing behind the trunk of his car counting quarters, nickels, and one-dollar bills for gas money. I felt sorry for him and his family out on the road on Independence Day, short on funds, but trying to get to his destination safely. As I walked by, I dug in my pocket and pulled out some loose change—a ten-dollar bill, a few five-dollar bills, a twenty, and a bunch of one-dollar bills—and gave it to the young man. I did that for him because I knew what it felt like to be stuck out on the road, and I didn't want that to happen to the young man and his family.

When I filled up my truck, I had to go back into the store to get the rest of the money I paid for the gas because my truck didn't take all of it. When I received the rest of the money, I walked by the young man's car, gave the change to his wife or girlfriend, told them, "Happy Fourth of July," and continued on with my road trip.

As we started our remaining 198-mile road trip, I had a chance to recap all the events that occurred with the truck and how I handled it. I have to say dealing with the tow truck guy who added more problems to the situation, I was about two seconds away from allowing my anger to get the best of me and let the tow truck guy see the worst side of me. On the upside, the hotel welcomed my family and me with open arms and allowed me to get my truck fixed on their property. My brother (bless his heart) found the energy to drive four hundred miles with a new battery and alternator. Another thing is I was able to help someone out in need at the gas station so they wouldn't be in the same situation as me being stuck out on the road with their family. Last but not least, I was still able to keep moving forward to take my wife to see her auntie for the first time in eighteen years in Lewiston, Idaho.

We finally arrived at my wife's aunt's house. It was a long journey due to the car trouble that I was so glad to have overcome. As I walked into to Auntie's house, it was like walking back in time. You could tell that back in the early eighties, the house was top of the line. The house had a self-cleaning, 1980s-style electric stove, which you could tell was a popular appliance back then, along with a full-sized refrigerator with double doors and an ice and water dispenser. All the appliances, and the kitchen cabinets, and countertops were original from when the house was built. As much as I would love to remodel the kitchen and bring it to the modern style, that kitchen was a classic. There was nothing to be done with the kitchen since everything was functioning correctly. Besides, it brought back memories of a similar house I used to live in when I was a little boy.

In the living room, there was a big front window with eighties window drapes along with the original carpet, still in good shape. The only thing that was modern in that living room was a flat-screen TV. In fact, the flat-screen TV was extremely out of place, but that was okay because the TV station that Auntie watched had nothing but old-school TV shows that I used to watch back in the mid-seventies and early eighties.

For the first time, I was fully content, and everything I needed was in Auntie's house. I sat back and watched all the old-school TV shows while my wife, mother-in-law, and Auntie chatted and caught up. Being at Auntie's felt like being stuck in the eighties, which worked out great for me because it really helped me remember how my childhood used to be. Besides the ass whooping I used to get when I was a little boy, childhood was pretty fun. Watching the old TV shows helped me remember what was going on in my lifetime then. I remembered the friends I had in school and the neighborhood kids I used to play with on Curtis Street in Berkeley, California.

Enjoying the precious time remembering my childhood, I never once thought about Iraq. Not one second. With that being said, I know if I am having a bad day or having issues with my PTSD, I know where I will go—Auntie's house in Lewiston, Idaho.

Besides using the house as my save haven, Lewiston had some good places for fishing—there was a nice river running beside the town. The 1980-style home and fishing spots created a good recipe for my coping skills.

Two days later, we loaded up in the hemi, along with Auntie, and headed 160 miles north to see my wife's cousin in Sand Point, Idaho. Sandpoint is a small town with a beautiful lake and log cabin homes. The temperature was about eighty-five degrees, and the lake had a little stretch of beach, which was nice. I waded in the icy water. It was fun; I almost felt like a kid again. Normally when I came to an unknown place, I would be in a hypervigilant mode watching everyone's moves. But since Sand Point was the type of place to have fun and enjoy water sport activities like fishing, scuba diving, partying on a boat, or riding on jet skis, I didn't have any triggers from Iraq. If I had some serious cash on my hands, Sand Point would be my summer vacation spot. It could be my place for therapy.

The next day, we left Sand Point with my wife's cousin. Our stay was short due to time constraints. I guess you can say we did a turn and burn, something that happened a lot with the unit from 84th

Engineer Battalion in Mosul, Iraq, in 2008 and 2009. I've been on one of the turn-and-burn missions, kind of crazy if you ask me. But being in Sand Point, Idaho, it was okay.

When we returned to Auntie's house, I had to admit I was kind of tired of being behind the wheel and I was happy to be back at her house. I wanted to get back to watching those old TV shows. The ladies were tired but were very happy and excited about the trips we made. The next day, the ladies went shopping in Lewiston, but I stayed at the house to enjoy the feeling of being in the eighties-style home and watching old movies. I even took a nap, woke up, and watched more old movies well into the night. I guess nothing outside of that living room bothered me. I was focused on enjoying the moments of watching the old movies and remembering the things that were going on back in the mid-70s and early 80s.

The third day, we decided to head back home to Syracuse, Utah. We talked about how nice the trip was and how Auntie stayed in that house all those years and never changed anything. That was okay because that house was a classic in my book. The hemi ran great on our trip home, and once we got home we got some much-needed rest. I made two other road trips, but the last road trip was another adventure back to California.

Third and Final Road Trip of Summer 2014

My last trip consisted of traveling 650 miles back to Fairfield, California, to catch a military flight from Travis Air Forces Base to Hickam Air Force Base in Honolulu, Hawaii. My intent was to talk with a few wounded Soldiers who were dealing with PTSD to give them a heads up that the battle is not over after leaving the Wounded Warrior Transition Program. I wanted them to be aware of more treatments for PTSD and keeping track off their benefits, like CRSC for those who qualify for Combat-Related Special Compensation (CRSC). Basically, I just wanted to let the Wounded Warriors know they still had a long road ahead of them after leaving the WTB. I also wanted to thank our group session counselors for educating us Soldiers on PTSD and developing coping skills to help with our issues. I believe that counselors should receive feedback from Soldiers who spend time in their group session to see what is working, what's not working, and understand why they're still struggling. I guess we should do something like "Where are they now?" after being in the WTB; that way we can have a big picture on how everyone is doing with their PTSD issues.

My plans for being in Hawaii didn't work out too well after driving 650 miles to Fairfield. During the month of August 2014, Hawaii had a bad hurricane that hit the islands. All military flights to Hawaii were canceled for four straight days; I tried to get on a flight, but no luck.

Despite the fact that I did not make the trip to Hawaii, the 650-mile road trip to Fairfield wasn't a waste of time. I decided to hang out with Mama Jenkins and the rest of the family. The Jenkins family had been like my second family. Back in the day, Mama Jenkins made sure that our asses were in school. Even though my good buddy, Brother Jenkins (her son) and I had a part-time job working at Church's Fried Chicken on North Texas Street, she made sure we were involved in a summer work program for the youth. I believe the purpose of Momma Jenkins keeping us kids gainfully employed was to keep us from not getting involved with street thugs or drug dealers. With two jobs during the summertime, we learned how it felt to make our own money, how to have a savings account, and how to buy our own school clothes with our own money. Mama Jenkins is an old-school parent who didn't take any shit from anyone. She kept us in line and busy, but as teenage boys, Brother Jenkins and I still found time to chase girls.

During my visit at Mama Jenkins' house, it really put me back in my high-school days with the same fun, laughter, and old stories that would make me laugh so much that my stomach hurt, and I loved every minute of it. I was so into the moment of what was going on at the house that I forgot I was retired from the Army. I forgot that I did four tours to Iraq, and I even forgot that I lived in Utah. Being at the house with all the fun and laughter really helped me reclaim my soul, the soul that was lost during the war. Mama Jenkins' house helped bring back Jocephus Duckworth, the person who I was back in the day, always smiling and full of jokes, the man who was carefree. I remember the days when I used to come to the house after having a bad day, but I would always leave the house with a smile and positive outlook on life.

I took time out to go to my favorite fishing spot at Grizzly Island. Things had changed since the early 1990s, but my fishing time was fun even though I didn't catch anything. I ran across an old Army Veteran who was out fishing. We spent about three hours swapping stories about our time in the service and shared information about VA benefits. That was the only time I was reminded of being a retired Veteran. I went back to the fishing spot three or four different times. I did the early morning fishing and late night fishing. One of the nights I went fishing, I was at another fishing spot that was farther than I normally went. There were a few people out fishing, but I felt a sense that I needed something to protect myself at that moment. I wished I had had a handgun or, better yet, my M4.

I guess being out at night brings out the Iraq war fighter in me. The only protection I had was my twenty-two-ounce framing hammer that I kept beside me while fishing. In the back of my truck, I had nothing but construction tools. I even hooked my air hose up to my air compressor. I figured if someone wanted to jack me for my truck and try to harm me because I was alone, if they get close enough, they would get three nail shots to the chest. The city of Fairfield was not the friendly town it was back in the seventies, eighties, and nineties. Over the years, most of the thug life and drugs just ransacked the town, which caused me to stay in a defensive mode. In other words, you can't walk down the street and say hello to a person without that person asking if you had ten bucks. In that situation, your best bet is just to say no and keep it moving, because if you stop, then you just set yourself up to get robbed. Situations like this go on all day, every day while living in places like Fairfield, Oakland, and Richmond.

This would explain how when I was at Momma Jenkins' house, I would stay inside the house unless she wanted me to go to the store, but then when I went I came straight back. I didn't stop anywhere. When I went fishing at some of the fishing spots at Grizzly Island, I texted Ed (Momma Jenkins' husband) and let him know which fishing spot I was at and when I was ready to head back to the house. It was about a fifteen-minute drive, but if something happened to me at least he could track down my last location.

After my sixth or seventh day, I decided to drive down to Southern California to see my buddy Brother Jenkins. Before I started my trip, I drove down to see my mom in Alameda. My relationship wasn't that great with my mom when as I was growing up. My mother was a pill addict back in the day. My daddy had to get most of her pills from the streets. When my dad passed away in July 2009, I had to fly from Mosul to Oakland, California, to help with funeral arrangements. When I saw my mom for the first time in years, I could tell she was strung out on whatever pills she was on.

Mom had trouble completing a full sentence and, at times, I believed she even forgot that Daddy had passed away. I also think she forgot that I flew from Iraq for the memorial service.

The day before the memorial service, Mom was so out of it that she called the police and said that her son had stolen her car. When I first heard about what she did, my brother and I were at the store—walking distance from her home—so I kind of laughed it off and never gave it any thought. Twenty minutes went by and my sister called me again to tell me that Mama made a second call to the police department about me stealing her car. As my sister was telling me this, I could tell in her voice that she wasn't playing. I told her that I never touched Mama's car except when I took her to her doctor's appointment two days prior.

When my brother and I arrived back at the house, I tried to talk to my mom to get an understanding of why she called the police. She never responded. She had a pen and paper and was trying to write something but couldn't write one letter because she was so high on her pills. Several police cars arrived to the house and my mom seemed to come out of her high stage and blasted out that her son stole her car. The officer could tell that I had that look like, "This is bullshit." For some reason, I got the sense that the police officer wasn't taking that car theft too seriously. The officer asked if I could come outside and talk to him. I went outside and informed him that I was in the Army and had flown from Iraq to deal with funeral affairs because my dad had passed way. He said he noticed that Mr. Duckworth wasn't sitting in his chair. I was surprised that the officer knew my parents by name. I told him that I never stole my mom's car and somehow he believed me.

He came back into the house and told my mother if she ever misused 911 calls again she would be going to jail. I was happy about what he said, but when the officers left I had a mouthful of nasty words for her. I mean at this point, I had lost all respect for my mother, and she really caught the wrath of Sergeant Duckworth. I don't know what came over me, but I guess the four tours in Iraq were taking their toll, along with Daddy passing away. Plus, she had been addicted to prescription pills all these years, and it felt like everything was crashing down. The whole family had a chance to see the worst side of Post-Traumatic Stress Disorder, which I didn't know anything about at that time. All six of her grandkids, her two sons and daughter, along with my wife, all saw the worst side of me. I believed all of them were scared and didn't know what to do to calm me down.

I had so much hatred toward my mother at that time that I had thoughts of putting duct tape around her mouth, taping her hands and feet inside those heavy-duty garbage bags, putting her in the garbage bag alive, then taking her to the end of the Berkeley Pier and dumping her in the ocean. What stopped me from acting on my emotions was thinking that she was my brothers' and sister's mother, as well as the kids' grandmother. If I acted on my emotions and thoughts, it would be a selfish act on my part. The sad thing was going to jail was the least of my worries.

So fast-forward five years when I visited my mom in Alameda in 2014. It was a surprise visit for my mom, and she was looking a lot better than when I saw her in July 2009. I could tell that she was kicking the pill addiction and carrying a good conversation. She even asked important questions about PTSD, and I learned that she did some research on PTSD. I shared some of my struggles with PTSD and talked about what I had done in Iraq. Mom cried when I told her that I spent six years running back and forth to Iraq, but she was happy that I had retired. I mean that is something that she could have her head held up high about, that her son fought for this country and now her son was retired. Some parents in the Bay Area are proud of their sons for getting out of prison after ten years of hard time and have the nerve to throw a welcome home party, like that's something to be proud of.

As I visited my mom, I have to say that I was glad I had my little episode in July 2009 with my mother because after all my group sessions with PTSD, I learned that having so much hatred does nothing but cause bodily harm to yourself. Muscles tighten up, and that can lead to a stroke or heart attack. Having overwhelming hatred takes up so much energy that it is truly exhausting by the end of the day or end of the week. I learned so much from my PTSD group sessions that I did not even waste time thinking about what my mother did in the past. I was just happy that when I visited my mother, we could have a healthy conversation.

After my visit, I finally made my journey south to meet up with Brother Jenkins and his family. It had been years since I was on Highway 5 heading south. The last time had been in 2001, while driving toward Magic Mountain with my brother and my wife. Before then, it was back in the seventies or eighties. As I drove on Highway 5, tearing up the roads with the big hemi, my memories of being on Highway 5 as a little boy came very clearly. I remembered the speed limit was fifty-five, but Daddy drove up to ninety heading toward Lemoore from Oakland. My brother and I acted as the radar detector by using binoculars and looking far ahead for highway patrol sitting at the overpass and looking out the back window for highway patrol in the back of a brown '77 Pontiac station wagon with a 454 Oldsmobile engine and four-barrel carburetor.

My old memories still continued while driving on Highway 5 heading south. For 357 miles on Highway 5, I didn't give any thoughts about Iraq or the road repair missions, except once when I thought about how hot it was on the highway. The temperature was anywhere from ninety-seven to 103 degrees, though in Iraq, it was much hotter. As I hauled ass, I had seen newer cars on the side of the road with the hood up due to the engine overheating. I looked at my temperature gauge and the temperature never reached the middle mark. There had been times I wanted to stop and help some of the drivers, but I knew Highway 5 was the drug trafficking route, and I wasn't trying to get caught up in anyone's bullshit.

As I drove further down the highway, catching up on memories, I remembered a town called Los Banos that used to have one exit. I think I counted five or six exits this time. Towns like Los Banos were no longer mom-and-pop towns; they had become cities with multiple exits. The same situation occurred at the Lemoore exit. The Lemoore exit was the halfway point to the Magic Mountain Amusement Park.

In fact, at one point back in the day, you needed to fill up if you wanted to get over the Grapevine mountain pass with elevation of fifteen hundred feet of an uphill climb and winding road. The Grapevine is such a steep mountain to climb that if you're at a half a tank of gas starting at the base of the mountain, you won't make it up and over the top. I filled up at the Lemoore exit at the same gas station where my father used to fill up back in the day. Of course, things have changed over the years. I was excited to get back on Highway 5 heading south and allow the hemi to do what it does on the highway.

As I got closer to Bakersfield, I saw big signs next to the farmlands that said, "No water, no work." These were the farmlands that grew America's fruits and vegetables. I noticed the signs after passing Los Banos, but I didn't pay them any mind until later. I saw more of them and understood what the signs really meant. I remembered seeing or hearing about the California drought on the news a few months back, but to actually see it firsthand was jaw-dropping.

As a Veteran in a construction mind-set, I was really upset at our government for not creating infrastructure jobs by creating desalination plants to turn sea water into fresh water strictly used for the farmlands. I mentioned about desalination plants earlier in the book when I talked about the Hoover Dam Project on how it created jobs for people, bringing the country out of the Great Depression.

As I passed Bakersfield, seeing the Grapevine not too far ahead and seeing more and more vehicles pulled over due to overheating. I saw a sign that said, "Last chance for fill up for fuel," so I decided to get off the highway get at least two gallons of water just in case my truck overheated while climbing the Grapevine. When I got back on the highway, I was about to put the old hemi to the test on this mountain climb. I figured if there was any engine trouble, it would be on this mountain. The Grapevine was good for causing vehicles to blow out their head gaskets. As I started to climb at the base of the mountain, I saw three highway patrol cars getting on the highway. I said, "Shit, I can't let the hemi do what it wants to do." So I kept a safe distance behind. The way they were driving, however, made it seem like they were on another mission, because they moved through the mountain extremely fast. When I lost sight of them, I decided to let the hemi run. I pushed every bit of ninety miles an hour up through the mountain with no signs of the engine bogging down. I stayed on the far left lane, and drivers were nice enough to get out of the big hemi's way. I hauled ass so fast that I missed the exit sign heading to Magic Mountain. I got over the Grapevine with no trouble. The sun was setting and the whole view of Southern California became new to me, even though California was my home state. The furthest south I ever got was Magic Mountain. I relied on my GPS to help me get to my buddy's house, but it put me about fifty miles out of the way. Come to find out, my buddy's home address was so new that the new housing area only had about thirty houses built right off of Highway 15 heading north, which would explain why the GPS took me fifty miles out of the way. I'm just glad it didn't take me to Compton.

I finally arrived at Brother Jenkins' house. It was kind of late, but I was so happy to see my old high-school buddy and his family. For two days, we made plans to go fishing in parts of the California mountains. At one fishing spot, we fished at night. The weather was kind of windy, but late into the night everything was calm. In fact, it was almost too calm, like the calm before the storm. I noticed the stars in the sky along with a full moon glowing over the lake. It was a perfect night for fishing, but at the same time, being out in the dark did put me back in that Iraq combat mind-set for no reason. The hypervigilance was so intense that the ringing noise in my left ear was loud. Across the lake, about 250 meters, I saw two fishermen walking down from the side of the rocky trail heading toward the beach. I said to myself, *If I was on a night mission and if they were insurgents with weapons, I would have shot their asses.* They only thing that kept my emotions under control was that I was fishing with my boy Brother Jenkins. But because it was nighttime, my guard was constantly up. As a Soldier, I would protect whoever I was with the same way I would protect my fellow Soldiers with whom I served in Iraq.

The fishing trip went pretty well. We didn't catch anything, but we did get a few bites. One thing I noticed about being retired is that although it is nice, when you have old school friends who are still working, it's kind of hard to spend more time with them because they are civilians and have to work to make a living. Meanwhile, I had a retirement check coming in every month, which meant a full-time job was the last thing on my bucket list. What was on my bucket list was to incorporate more fishing time for myself. Fishing had always been fun, regardless of if I caught anything. The point of being out there is to feel free and have fun with your fishing buddies. From what I believe, fishing is therapeutic, which makes me understand why my dad loved fishing, especially deep-sea fishing. Since this past fishing trip, I had been thinking about catching a charter boat from Berkley Marina and heading out to the Farallon Islands to catch rockfish like red snapper and lingcod, something that Brother Jenkins and I used to do back in our high-school days.

On the third day, I started my trip heading home to Utah. Even though it was a short visit, I had fun hanging with my buddy and his family. Since the new housing area he lived in was right off of Highway 15 North, it was very easy to jump on the highway. But you can't head north without stopping in Vegas.

Driving 225 miles to Vegas was a nice ride—just the big hemi and me feeling carefree and the AC blowing because it was 103 degrees. When I arrived in Vegas, it was my second visit in my whole entire life. I'm not a gambler, but I stayed in Vegas just to see how well I did in crowded places. Casinos are a good spot to test anxiety and hypervigilance.

I stayed at The Orleans Hotel and Casino for three days. I never played a slot machine or poker. However, I did enjoy watching fellow Veterans, wearing their black Veteran's caps, play their favorite slot machines. I was hoping one of them would hit the jackpot because they deserved to win the big one after fighting for this country. One the things I saw that kind of made me upset, but that was funny at the same time, were a few elderly people with their walkers almost running me over trying to get to the slot machines. For the first time after three different therapy sessions with PTSD and anger issues, I knew there a change in me. Now, if I had been in Vegas in 2009 after coming home from Iraq, I believe the elderly people would have heard some nasty words coming from me.

On the second day at The Orleans, I went downstairs to see what activities they had to offer besides poker tables and slot machines. I saw a full range of bowling lanes. I believe they had forty or fifty lanes, and the lanes were occupied. I couldn't tell if there was a big bowling league going on or not. I figured if there was a bowling league going on, then each team would have uniforms or colored T-shirts with their team names and logos. I decided to get a large Pepsi and sit at one of the vacant chairs that overlooked the bowling activities. I sat next to a woman to whom I said hi and got a response with some attitude. A lot of people looked at me as if they were wondering what I was doing there. It triggered my defensive mode that I would have had if I were in Iraq, meaning I saw her as a threat if she continued to act this way. I think I sat there for ten minutes drinking my Pepsi, and then her friend showed up. She never spoke to me, not even a simple hello. So again, it put me in the defensive mode. My hypervigilance kicked in and the ring in my left ear started up again. They started whispering to each other as the woman stood directly behind me. I wanted to tell the lady not to stand behind me, but I knew by me being so keyed up and almost on edge, things could go south real fast, and I would be that black guy going to jail in Vegas. A few minutes went by and a young man and his little boy came on the left side of me and asked if the seat on the left was taken. I told him that I had been sitting there for about ten to fifteen minutes and no one had sat there since I had been there. I encouraged him to have a seat, but seconds later, the same woman who had been standing behind me told the young man that someone was sitting there.

I turned around and looked at her and her friend with a mean look on my face like what the fuck?? The two females never elaborated more on the situation. By this time, the inner rage that I thought I had a tight lid on was seconds away from coming out of me. I did the best I could to block it out so I could focus on the bowling games, but that damn woman still continued to stand right behind me, so I decided to leave and do something else.

Since I drank all my Pepsi, I decided to leave and throw my drink in the trash nearby. As I looked back, that same woman who was standing behind me for the entire thirty minutes sat in the seat where I had been sitting, even though there were five other seats open on my left side. I felt like I was surrounded by ignorant people and everyone was a threat. I continued to stay in a defensive mode since I was alone in that casino, wishing I had a "battle buddy" to be with me at times like this. I saw an arcade room that I thought would put me in a good mood. But out of all the fun arcade games, I picked a shooting game, a sniper game. While playing, I noticed I was still using the same shooting technique as if I was firing my M4 or M16 (site picture, breathing, aiming, trigger squeeze). As I was shooting, it was mostly head shots or chest shots for the first time, and I wasn't too happy. I was pissed off because I hadn't touched my weapon (M4) since 2009. Five years went by and I still carried the same shooting techniques as if I had never left Iraq. I stopped playing the game and allowed some young kid to play; I gave him the rest of my tokens.

After the arcade game, I ended up in my room. I used my room to calm down and try to make some sense of what was up with those two women at the bowling alley. The only thing I could think of was that they were self-centered, it was all about them, and they both had that "why are you talking to me"-type attitude. Now with that said, all I said to the lady who sat on my right was, "Hello, ma'am," and that was the end of my sentence. From there, that's when all the attitude started. Anyhow, I think I calmed down about four hours later. Somehow I found a movie theater inside the casino. I can't remember what I saw, but it was a good pastime while being alone. After the movies, I decided to fill the truck up that night so I could jump on the road to Utah in the morning.

The next morning, around eight or nine, I checked out of the room and finally got back on the road for the first time. I felt safe in my own truck. I guess because there was no verbal contact with people, just Big Hemi and me. Traffic was kind of heavy but I guess that could be normal around Vegas. Outside the city limits, I was able to allow the old hemi to do what it does on the highway. As I was driving, somehow I was triggered again. In other words, I was back in my convoy mind-set. I don't know what triggered it, but it was all a new territory that kept me feeling hypervigilant during my trip to Syracuse.

I quickly learned that hypervigilance was a good thing to have in a non-combat situation because it helped me pick out the highway patrol cars that liked to hide behind the metal guardrails out in the median or looking like a broken down vehicle on the side of the road. The hypervigilance helped me notice something far down the highway, even at traveling speeds of eighty to ninety miles per hour. I saw something out of place on the side of the road. I attempted to get out of the lane, and in this case it was a highway patrol vehicle that looked out of place, hiding low behind the guardrail. These highway patrol vehicles reminded me of vehicles on the side of the road in Iraq that were loaded down with IEDs. I stayed hypervigilant, triggered, and constantly in a convoy mind-set. None of my coping skills were working and none of the jazz songs I listened to put me in a better mind-set. The only thing that was working was that my truck was moving with a mean purpose. A hundred and forty miles later, I drove into Saint George, Utah. I didn't need gas at all—I still had three-quarters of a tank of gas, which would easily take me into Salt Lake City. But I thought about the time I would be rolling into Salt Lake; it would be traffic hour. I decided to add more gas so I would not have to get off the highway in Salt Lake. I could stay to the far left lane heading home to Syracuse.

While at the gas station filling up, I noticed this van. There wasn't anything special about it other than you could tell it contained a family on a road trip. But for some reason I had a bad feeling about the van. I don't know what you call it when you have a bad feeling about something and later you found out something bad did happen. Two hundred miles later, that van was flipped over, which explained the two-hour traffic on a desert highway. The last time I had that same feeling that something bad was about to happen was when I was working on a bathroom remodeling job on the west end of Honolulu on Alapaki Street.

I stopped at a corner store to get a Snickers bar and Pepsi. As I parked my truck, I noticed this Honda Accord. It truly gave me some bad vibes when I walked into the store and I scanned everyone, looking at them from head to toe. I did the same to the person who was working the cash register. Out of everyone in the store, this lady who was holding a baby and talking to the worker at the register gave me a bad vibe. The negative vibe was so strong, I wanted to tell her to stop running her mouth and just leave the store. She finally left as I was getting my items. I saw her getting into that gray Honda Accord and my first thought was, *How did I know that's her car?* When I paid for my items, I noticed that she was just now getting her and the baby in the car. I finally got into my truck and the woman in the Honda Accord was trying to get out of the parking area by making a left turn onto the main road, which was very difficult to do on the west end of the island. I tried to make a right turn, which was difficult as well. About three minutes went by and the woman was still trying to get out. A truck off the main road was trying to make a left turn into the parking lot of the convenient store, and about twenty seconds later, a driver traveling behind the truck slammed on his brakes and veered to the left that led him into oncoming traffic but veered off even more, hitting a posted sign. He hit the Honda Accord that had the women and the baby inside. When all this happened, I was inside my truck yelling at top of my lungs saying, "Shit, you motherfucker, if you wouldn't have been running your fucking mouth in the store, you wouldn't be in this situation." I hated myself for knowing that something bad was going to happen to that mother and the baby. Like I said, I don't know what you would call it when you know something bad is about to happen. In fact, I hate having those feelings. It is very exhausting and it keeps me hypervigilant looking for something bad to happen. I was so upset when that happened that I never made it to the bathroom remodel job; I just went home and locked myself in my bedroom. I didn't want see anyone, and I didn't want to see or hear anything that was going on outside. While in my room, I turned on the A/C just so it would block out the outside noise.

As I drove by the accident scene of the flipped-over van on Highway 15 heading northbound toward Salt Lake City, I knew that no one had survived. In fact, there were two body bags on that side of the road. Like I said before, I don't know why I had a bad feeling about that van as I was pumping gas in Saint George, and I don't know what to label the feeling when you know something bad is going to happen.

As I approached Salt Lake City, of course evening traffic had begun. As I mentioned before, I stayed to the far left and kept moving. At this point, I was about twenty miles from home when I reached Kaysville. I got off the highway and took the back country roads home. When I arrived on Antelope Drive to make a right turn, my gas light came on. There was a gas station right on the corner, but I kept going. I was less than a quarter of a mile from home. Now remember, I filled up in Saint George, 366 miles ago. I should have gotten four hundred miles on a tank of gas if I had not been stuck in traffic for two hours. When I arrived home, I felt like a mission had been accomplished. During that week being on the road, I realized I did an eighteen hundred-mile round trip. It was fun being on the road with just Big Hemi and me. It seemed like my truck was the only thing that came close to me having a battle buddy. Big Hemi kept me safe and it moved when it was time to move. Being in my truck was comforting and I wouldn't trade it in for anything in the world.

When winter set in, the hemi didn't take too kindly to the cold weather. I discovered that the oil pressure kept dropping, which never happened before, especially while on road trips. I know many places where I could have blown the engine and been be stuck on the side of the road. My brother told me that I should trade it in, but like I said this truck was my battle buddy. You don't just trade your battle buddy in for a new friend. I've taken the truck in for repairs, and I assumed the oil pump was going out, but come to find out the pickup tube was dirty and the oil pan had oil sludge with metal shavings inside. I don't know how long those metal shavings and oil sludge had been in the oil pan, but I knew I had kept up with the regular oil changes. But then again, when you buy a 2004 used truck in 2011 and later have it shipped to the mainland, you get what you get. I can say that even with the engine troubles it had it truly took care of me while on these road trips, just like a battle buddy you take care of in the battlefield. I know if I had ten to twelve grand, I would get a new engine and transmission only because that truck took care of me and I couldn't afford a new 2015 Dodge with all the bells and whistles. Furthermore, I enjoyed not having a truck payment. While my truck was in the shop, the mechanic replaced the pickup tube and cleaned out the oil pan. So far the hemi, with 171,000 miles, was still going strong. I believed that it would be ready for another road trip in the summer of 2015.

Prior to attending church, I remember a chaplain from the WTB at Schofield Barracks always talking about being resilient, meaning all Soldiers who suffered multiple trauma experiences from war can and will bounce back from their bad experiences. During that time, I didn't have a clue what the man was talking about when it came to us Soldiers being resilient. I mean I knew what the word *resilient* meant, but I didn't see that light at the end of the tunnel—to see that I was, in fact, resilient. As an individual with PTSD, I became so preoccupied with events in the past that it could be hard to imagine a future or that light at the end of the tunnel. I felt like that sheep I read about in the Holy Bible. "For you were like sheep going astray, but now you have returned to the Shepherd and Overseer of your souls" (1 Peter 2:25).

I couldn't see the small blessings that the Lord was giving me as I dealt with my issues from war. One of the blessings I recall was when I spent four years living in my condo and had not made a mortgage payment at all. When I was able to be back on active duty to work on my medical treatment for PTSD, I made enough money to start making the mortgage payments, but I was so far behind that I didn't make any efforts to make the payments. So with the money that I made, I made extra payments toward my wife's car as well as extra payments toward my truck. I did this because when I retired, I didn't have to worry about car payments, and I also knew that my retirement pay would be much less then what my active-duty pay was.

While on active duty, I had my wife take out $2,000 on the first of every month and $1,000 on the fifteenth of every month. We did that for a year straight while my wife and daughter lived with my mother-in-law, until I was able to come home. So when I retired, we would have money to rent a place in Utah. So overall those were the blessings that the Lord gave my family and me. I mean He truly kept us from being homeless. I have to say it had to be an act of God that our home wasn't foreclosed on. From what I've learned, God will provide you with an opportunity to help yourself out of a bad situation. I had to look at the small blessings that have led me toward the bigger blessings. One of my bigger blessings was that my family and I were not homeless. We had a roof over our heads, food to eat, three vehicles that were paid for, and our condo was sold on a short sell.

I was retired with all my benefits, and for the first time in 2015, I felt like Jocephus Josey Duckworth and not damaged goods from war, which means now I understand what the chaplain meant when he said that all Soldiers who suffered with multiple traumas from war can and will be resilient. Feeling resilient, I have to give thanks to the chaplain, all the staff at WTB, and most importantly give thanks to God that I'm not in jail. My two biggest fears in dealing with PTSD are being homeless and having the mind-set to cut someone's throat and not give a damn about what happened. Again, I give thanks to God for putting the right people in place for the proper treatment for PTSD and steering me away from evil that would have me locked up in jail. God is Good.

After having the feeling of being resilient and returning to church again, I had the strength to work on other issues about myself. One of the two things I wanted to work on was bringing spirituality back into my soul. As I look back on my tours to Iraq, I feel that war had ripped my soul to shreds. I mean, I lost the meaning of what humanity was. The only thing I knew during wartime was to complete the mission no matter what. In other words, failure was not an option. When you shoot, you shoot to kill. In order to survive war, you have to become war. Anything you think is normal in the American way of life needs to leave your consciousness in a wartime situation. If I saw a seven-year-old boy in Iraq carrying a mortar around, guess what? I would put a bullet in his head just so he wouldn't live to fight another day and kill my fellow Soldiers. A normal civilian would see that same seven-year-old boy in Iraq carrying a mortar round and think that little boy was carrying a metal object, not knowing that the little boy was out to kill Soldiers.

So to repair my soul, I needed to regain spirituality. I feel that spirituality fuels the soul. Spirituality creates an inner belief system providing an individual with meaning and purpose in life, a sense of the sacredness of life, and a vision for the betterment of the world. In my case, I believe that my sole purpose in life is to enjoy life and the people around me. I also aim to use my construction skills that I learned while enlisted in the US Army and employ the seven Army Core Values in taking care of my fellow Veterans and other service members. In other words, I need to protect my fellow Veterans from shady money-hungry contractors who like to do a half-ass jobs and take the money and run. I'm sick of these useless contractors screwing over our service members and their family's dream home. From what I've gathered from homeowners, it seems like there's a pure lack of integrity and selfless service with these shady contractors, and this is the main reason why I understand my new calling, which is to protect the homeowners. I'm here to make a change.

God Put You in Peoples' Lives for a Reason

The Christian church that my wife found eighteen months prior to me coming to Utah has a congregation of people with whom I have become good friends. My newfound friend is in the Army just like I was, so as fellow service members, we began to share Army stories. As the months went by with us attending church, my fellow service members informed me that his neighbor that lived on base had been having trouble with two other contractors who didn't complete the home remodeling on his dream home in Syracuse, Utah.

The sad part was the Master Sergeant (Air Force) was deployed to the Middle East, which left his wife and two kids, ages eighteen months and eight years, to look at the ruins of their dream home. Prior to meeting with the Master Sergeant's wife at the unlivable home, I decided to bring my mother-in-law to look at the terrible house with me. When we arrived to the house, the house didn't look like a family home; it looked like an abandoned home. The home looked out of place in a nice neighborhood, and the landscape was growing out of control. The inside of the house was mostly unfinished. I mean there was a lot of incomplete stuff that the contractors didn't finish. There was so much unfinished stuff that I didn't know where to start. I believed that the kitchen was the worst. In fact, the Master Sergeant and his wife didn't have a kitchen.

After the awful tour of the five-bedroom, three-bath, forty-five-hundred-square-foot home, it took me a good two hours to absorb all the bad craftsmanship and unfinished jobs in order for me to come up with a good game plan to tackle the problems and turn this house around to a livable home. The Master Sergeant's wife was so sick of what had happened to her home that she was in tears. I was glad that my mother-in-law was there to comfort her because I personally didn't know what to do or what words to say to comfort her other than saying that everything would be all right. I know that was an understatement for her because she couldn't see the potential of a newly finished home when she was surrounded by ruins. But somehow I could see it. My mother-in-law continued to give her comfort because the Master Sergeant's wife was still in tears. She told her that if anyone could turn this house around it would be me. In the back of my mind, I thought, *I don't know if I can pull this one off.* It was a very tall order and tons of work to get to the finished product, but as a Construction Engineer Soldier from the United States Army, I never did a job that I couldn't finish.

In the Construction Engineer field, there were two famous sayings that I always heard during construction: "Make it happen," and, "Get 'er done." Not to mention the 84th Engineer Battalion motto: "Never Daunted." In other words, I wasn't going to allow this home project to intimidate me. So as you can see, I couldn't back away from this job, especially while Master Sergeant was deployed to the Middle East and was praying for a miracle back at home. The way I see it, you take care of your fellow service members in wartime as well as at home. The same American civilians that you put your life on the line to protect can be enemies as well. So we as service members and Veterans have to protect and help one another, and that's what I've done for the Master Sergeant and his family.

In August 2014, I was more than happy that a home remodel job required the skills I had gained throughout my experience in the United States Army. Before I started the projects, I wanted to ensure the Master Sergeant I was the man for the job. I sent him pictures of construction projects I had done in the Army as well as kitchen remodels and bathroom remodels. When the Master Sergeant saw all the pictures, he e-mailed me and said I would be the guy to work on future projects at his home. I had been retired from the Army since November 2013 from Schofield Barracks Hawaii. Since then, I had been to job fair after job fair, and no one gave me the time of day to work in the construction field. Why does it take a Veteran to understand one's skills and put him to work? These civilian companies did not seem to understand that the US Army has

Construction Engineer Soldiers. But the Master Sergeant in the Air Force understood my skills. I'm so blessed that he put me to work, gave me a sense of purpose, and allowed me to understand my self-worth.

Let the Home Remodel Begin

As I mentioned before, the unfinished bad craftsmanship was hard to absorb. My first game plan was to tackle all the walls (living room, kitchen, eating area). Everywhere I looked there was some type of crazy problem with these walls. I didn't know what type of wall texture the contractor was trying to apply on the walls, but it was a hot mess. I'm talking about a total of fifteen hundred square feet of walls that were damaged with poor wall texture. I ended up using my electric sander and sanding every bit of square footage just to smooth out the walls. Later I had to get the bucket of mud "joint compound" and spread it over all the walls just to cover the deficiencies.

After the mud dried for twenty-four hours, I sanded the walls again to achieve the smooth look on the walls. Once the all the walls were free from all deficiencies, it was time to apply primer. I put two coats of primer on all of the walls. The next day, the painting began with two different colors of yellow. One yellow color was for the living room and the other was for the kitchen and the little eating area. I put two coats of paint for each color. When the painting was completed, I was so relieved that half the battle was won. I did five different tasks (sanding, mud, sanding, primer, painting) to achieve the finished product on the walls. It was a daunting task but I pushed forward to get the job done. Even though there was a lot of work to be done with the walls, and it was extremely tiring, I got up each morning with an extreme sense of purpose in life. As I worked on the walls, I listened to smooth jazz. This helped me focus on the job without having massive thoughts running through my mind at a hundred miles per hour. It also helped me plan out how I would solve future work problems on the house.

The Master Sergeant's wife saw how nicely the two colors she picked out for the walls turned out. For the first time, she was able to see the light at the end of the tunnel. But also since there was fresh paint on the walls, she could see the other problems that would be an eyesore if I didn't take care of them. The other deficiencies I needed to tackle were the countertops, backsplash for the kitchen sink, and stove area. I also needed redo the carpentry work that was left undone by the contractor, replace all trim work around the French door and window, and create a shelving system for the new pantry.

The next task was to replace the countertops and backsplash. I was required by the Master Sergeant to take out the poorly installed countertop the contractor had done. The Master Sergeant and his wife liked my recommendation of having solid pieces of Silestone for the backsplash behind the stove area and kitchen sink. Silestone was also used for the countertops in the kitchen. I couldn't do the job myself because I did not have the tools, and I was not licensed or bonded to handle the Silestone material. As a retired Staff Sergeant from the US Army, this was the part where I used my Construction Management Skills to outsource some additional help to make the countertop and backsplashes a successful completion.

I went to Home Depot to talk to their kitchen and design people like I always did for all my kitchen and bathroom remodels regarding cost estimates for installation and the cost of the Silestone materials. I did whatever I could to help keep the cost down and not hurt the Master Sergeant's pocketbook. I helped save money by choosing a bull-nose finish that still created a fancy finished edge look but that was still cost effective.

There was a sale promotion going on for the Silestone I picked, and the promotion was that they received a free kitchen sink. Later, I e-mailed the Master Sergeant the cost of the countertops and the backsplash for the stove and kitchen sink. Normally, it was an eight-hour turnaround for an e-mail response from him since he was in the Middle East.

On the next day, I got the green light. The cost estimates were in his price range, but I had to wait again, due to the time difference, for the Master Sergeant to make the call from the Middle East to pay for the Silestone countertops at Home Depot. When the transaction was complete, I was able to make plans to set up an installation date. A week and a half later the countertop installers arrived to the house and installed the countertops and backsplash.

During this time, the Master Sergeant's wife didn't have to be there for the installation or planning of the countertops. I was the project manager throughout the whole process of getting their house turned around. When the countertop installation was complete, Master Sergeant's wife was pleased with the new countertops along with the backsplash and the free sink. She saw that the project was turning around and moving in a forward direction, but she saw more work ahead that needed to be done, like landscaping. I was not a landscaper, but I got a hold of a fellow Veteran who ran a small landscaping business. I figured since he cut my grass, I could take the time to help him build his clientele by sending him to my father-in-law's house to cut his grass and trim bushes.

I had him come out to the Master Sergeant's house to give an estimate and a vision of how he could turn their yard around to make it well groomed. The landscaper was hired by the Master Sergeant to landscape the front and backyard. Three big trees were cut down. Since the landscaper was working on the yard, he ended up getting another client three houses down. I was happy for him because my efforts of helping a fellow Veteran grow his business were paying off. I always say that we Veterans have to help one another in any way we can. Since our government seems not to care to create jobs for us, I feel it's my duty to help create jobs for all Veterans who come into my life. The landscaper gained six clients since he met me, and he had two more clients in spring 2015. Like I said, I love helping fellow Veterans with jobs because I know how hard it is to find a job.

The next task was to do something for the breakfast bar. The Master Sergeant's wife wanted a wooden butcher-block countertop for the breakfast bar. I traveled sixty miles south to a woodcraft shop to purchase the butcher-block countertop. It ended up being a special order so it took a few weeks to arrive to the shop. During that time, I was able to work on other tasks. The Master Sergeant's wife decided that she wanted same matching ceramic tiles on the floor to be cut in half and used as the baseboard throughout the living room, kitchen, and eating area. So 125 tiles were cut down to five inches, of which I was able to get two cuts out of one tile. Ultimately, 250 five-inch by twelve-inch tiles were installed throughout the perimeter of the walls to be used as ceramic tile baseboards. The tile work was a tedious with countless hours spent on my hands and knees installing and grouting the baseboard tiles. For the first time, I understood what "labor of love" meant.

As I continued to wait for the butcher-block countertop to come in, I had a surprising task to conquer. The Master Sergeant's wife decided that her master bedroom closet just wasn't working for her. As many times as I had been at that house working, I never gave the master bedroom closet any thought, but I took a few minutes to look at what was not working for her and decided that she was right. The closet wasn't working for her. The master bedroom closet had nothing but shelves and no place to hang clothes at all. I asked her who created this closet and she said the contractor did. I told her that all the shelving had to come out in order for me to give her a closest space with shelving and a place to hang her clothes.

Once again, I had to coordinate with the Master Sergeant to buy the materials at Home Depot. Due to military pay being on the first and the fifteenth of each month, I had to wait until then to pick up the materials. In the meantime, I was able to take out the old shelving, do some wall repairs, and later some painting. I was lucky enough to have a little money to purchase two recess lights for the closet. I chose the daylight bright light because in small spaces like closets and pantries, the area needs all the bright light it can get. When the Master Sergeant had the funding to pay for the closet remodel, I chose the Closet Maid and shelf track adjustable organizational system, which turned out to be very functional. I used the same organizational system for the pantry. When the master bedroom closet was complete, the wife was very pleased with how the Closet Maid shelf track adjustable organization system turned out and loved the idea of how I installed the two recess lights using the daylight lightbulbs. She immediately brought their clothes from the other house on base to be hung in the new closet.

The Master Sergeant's wife could see the light at the end of the tunnel, but I saw in her eyes that she was still emotionally scarred from what the two previous contractors had done to their home. I remember her mentioning to me that after what has happened, prior to me working on the house, she still saw the house as a house instead of a home. She had come from Italy to the United States, and she was given a bad representation of how the American people conducted business. Throughout the project, I did my best to put out the best quality work on her home and made sure I did whatever she asked me to do. I hoped that I worked hard enough to change her heart and mind that not all American people were bad. I also hoped she would see her house as a home after I was done with all the work.

The butcher-block countertop finally arrived from the woodcraft shop down in Sandy, Utah. Of course, I had to drive back down to get it. The butcher-block was much longer than I thought, but it worked out to my favor since it was seven feet long by thirty-two inches wide. I was able to cut it down to size and use the scrap pieces to sand down the varnish that the manufacturer put on the butcher-block. During this time at the Master Sergeant's house, I turned their two-car garage to a woodworking workshop. Like I said earlier, I used the scrap pieces to sand down and use the router to create a bull-nose look on the edges on each side of the butcher-block and then sanded it down more to be super smooth. The scrap piece was ready for the two coats of pre-stain conditioner, then later I added the natural wood stain. I liked using the natural wood stain because it brought out the natural color of the wood. I could add the natural stain to the wood until I got the color that I was looking for. A day later, I was able to apply the polyurethane, or "clear gloss." I used three coats of polyurethane to bring out the high gloss shine. When I presented the sample pieces to the Master Sergeant's wife, she was pleased with the sample pieces. I've learned throughout my years of woodworking (carpentry work), it is best to have a scrap piece to work to see how the finished product will turn out.

I spent $297 for the butcher-block countertop, and I had no choice but to have a scrap piece to work on before the actual working piece. When I was ready to work on the actual piece, I remembered a few flaws that I created on the scrap piece, but I made sure that I would do a better job on the main product. The butcher-block countertop turned out better than the sample pieces. I was lucky enough to use the router-to-router out of the butcher-block underneath, so it could recess into the short wall for the breakfast bar. When I installed the butcher-block countertop as a breakfast bar, it made the kitchen complete, along with the finished carpentry work I did for the wall that wasn't tied to the ceiling. I guess the breakfast bar was the icing on the cake to make the kitchen a functioning kitchen. During the time I was working on the breakfast bar out in the garage, I also worked on other wood trim pieces that required wood staining and polyurethane around the window and French door.

At this stage, everything was winding down. At the end of the project, the wife came up with a plan for me to apply some sealer on her tile floors. I was glad she mentioned about sealing the tile floors because I could see right off the bat that the last contractor didn't seal the tile floors after the ceramic tile installation. I decided to take it a step further and apply the high gloss sealer. The high gloss sealer made the floor look constantly wet. I applied three coats of high gloss sealer over nine hundred square feet of flooring and tile baseboards, using a three-inch sponge brush. Sealing the floors was done just in time for the movers to move in all furniture two days later.

I had two days to pack up tools and turn the woodshop back into a two-car garage. My good friend from church saw the transformation of the house and said God was working with me to make all this happen. She said the work I had done was better quality than a contractor. I told her that it was my duty to give the customer what he or she wanted and to give the best quality work I could. Our pastor even came by to look at finished work. I was glad the pastor came and visited the house because then he had a chance to see why I missed so many church services. I told the pastor that I felt it was my duty to help another service member by getting his home back together for him and his family. The pastor smiled. He could see that the Lord was working in me while completing the home remodel.

The pastor then asked me if I was a licensed contractor. I was offended because he knew that I did construction in the United States Army. I told him that all the work done to this house was cosmetic. In other words, I gave the house a "face lift." Since I was offended by the question from the pastor, I had a funny question for him. I asked him when God asked Noah to build an ark for God's people and all the animals, did He question Noah if he was a licensed contractor to build an ark?

The pastor had a funny look on his face and said that those were different times back then. I told the pastor that God sent me to this house to help the family with their distress, but I believed that God wouldn't send me out to do something if God thought I didn't know what I was doing. But like I said in the beginning, God will put you in peoples' life for a reason. The reason He put me in the Master Sergeant's life was to provide my construction management skills and trade skills to turn his house around to be a livable home for his family.

Bad Vibe in the Neighborhood

Between August 2014 and November 2014, I worked on that house daily. The part that bothered me the most was that I always felt unwelcome in the neighborhood. I suspect the neighborhood was 80 percent Mormon, due to the fact that the there was a Mormon church in the neighborhood. Every Sunday that I was at the house working, I saw people from the neighborhood walking to and from their church as I was working in the garage and doing some woodworking. Not one person would stop to say hi or wave hello. Some just looked at me with dumb looks on their faces, probably wondering why I was in their neighborhood or if I lived there. Now I knew damn well they knew what had happened to that house prior to me working on the house.

Since the Master Sergeant's wife was from Italy and she was Catholic, no one in the neighborhood would give her the time of day to be her friend or help her with anything she needed for her house. I wondered what the hell happened to helping thy neighbor. The things I saw gave me a bad vibe about the neighborhood, and my war mind-set started to set in. I figured that everyone in the neighborhood was a threat to me since they couldn't say hello or take the time to meet me and see what I had done to the house. But then again, even if they had seen my fine work, they might be intimidated about the quality of work I had done, not to mention that a black man had turned this house around. Yet if I was white and part of the Good Old Boys Club at the Mormon Church, I would be the neighborhood hero that turned that house around. I know at this point, it seemed like I had something against Mormons, but I didn't; it's just that I didn't know where their heads were, and I didn't understand some of their beliefs.

What I do know is that the Mormon followers, as well as any other religious followers, need to understand that Americans have the freedom to follow or worship any religion they wish to practice. Try practicing the Mormon religion in Mosul. You best believed that your head will be cut off at noon. So with that said, it truly made me mad when I saw these Mormon followers in the neighborhood with their noses up in the air, only worrying about their little lives and their circle of friends and church.

Meanwhile, there was a Master Sergeant in the Air Force who had been deployed to the Middle East and had to deal with the ISIS crap. At the same time, there was me, a Veteran who had done four tours to Iraq, fighting for and protecting America's freedom. I took time out to help turn the Master Sergeant's house around. Meanwhile, the people in the neighborhood walked around with their noses up in the air. No one stopped to see what they could do to "help thy neighbor." Shame on you people! I guess what I'm getting at is, can we put our differences aside like religion, race, color, and any other differences to achieve a common goal like helping a neighbor in distress? Recognize the service members who are out fighting and protecting your freedom and understand what it takes to protect your freedom. Remember, the United States is the only place where you can worship any religion as you wish and not have to worry about getting your head cut off. God Bless America and the service members and Veterans who fought and died for America's freedom.

Being in the Wrong Place

God will let you know when you are in the wrong place for His services. When I was done working on the house, I felt like I needed a full-time job. I thought if I had a full-time job, I could be part of society, Plus I wanted to tackle some of the bad things that were on my credit so that I would be able to purchase a home two years down the road.

I applied for a sandblasting position at a company that built fifty-foot tractor-trailers. I chose the sandblasting position because for the past month, my brother, who worked for the same company, told me how they had these young eighteen-year-old kids working in the sandblasting booth, spending their whole time on their phones. I told my brother that the work ethics of young men today were terrible, especially when they only worked a ten-hour shift for four days—but during the four days they would want to call in sick. In my opinion, you can't rely on them. In fact, I don't know how businesses stay in business these days.

Like I mentioned earlier, I applied for the sandblasting position, thinking that my strong work ethics from the Army would help get things done and add little more profit in the company's pockets. A week later, I was scheduled for a job interview. During the interview, we talked about my experience in the military and what my responsibilities were as a supervisor in the United States Army. I explained how I truly wanted to be a sandblaster for the company and help the sandblasting section get some parts done because when you have parts waiting to get sandblasted, that means that the customers who are paying for the new trailers have to wait. The company making the trailers would miss their deadline and lose some of the profits when parts were not sandblasted in a timely manner.

I thought the interview went well. I was asked to take a drug test, which, as a retired service member, I never had a problem passing. Two days went by and I had to attend the eight-hour orientation for all new employees. During the orientation, I had to listen to all the medical benefits that the company had to offer. I later told them that I would not need their medical benefits because I paid $546 bucks a year for my family and me. The guy who was in charge of the orientation asked me how I managed to get that medical plan. I told him that I served my country and that was what I have to pay for medical while being retired. Throughout the orientation, I learned that my starting pay was so low that I would make more money sitting on retirement than I did going to work, but I really didn't care because I really wanted to make an impact on downsizing the backlog of parts waiting for sandblasting.

On a Monday, I started the night shift from 3:30 p.m. to two o'clock in the morning, four nights a week. At times, we worked overtime until four and worked eight hours overtime on Fridays. Compared to the crazy work hours in Iraq, the work schedule was nothing, but I could tell some civilians who worked the same shift looked like they were hurting and dragging ass. I had to shake my head and say to myself, *If only they knew what real work is.* I bet half of them wouldn't last one day in Iraq, yet they claimed to be hard workers.

On the first night on the job, I was shocked because I was all hyped up to work in the sandblasting booth and looking to get some stuff done, but somehow I ended up working in a whole different work area. The other work section consisted of building fifty-foot long panel walls by installing rivets in the holes to create the panels. I did that job for about two weeks and was transferred over to another work section that required me to spot clean the trailers walls before they went out the door. The supervisor issued me a spray bottle of Simple Green, a spray bottle of water, green scrubbing pads, and some rags. When I was assigned to clean the trailers, I knew I had to only spot clean, like getting any scuff marks off the trailers. But I took it a step further by cleaning every square foot of the exterior walls of the trailers.

When I cleaned the aluminum panels using Simple Green, the scrubbing pad left scratchy marks on the aluminum panels, but I sprayed the aluminum panels with water and wiped them clean, using the rags. When I looked at the aluminum panels after I cleaned them, the aluminum panels almost looked like chrome. I continued doing the same process and it caught a few peoples' attention, including the supervisor. The supervisor told me that he had never seen anyone put so much effort into cleaning. He asked me if I liked to clean and I told him no, but it had to be done.

I also told him I was a retired Soldier and my cleaning habits were still embedded in me even after being retired for a year. I told him that most Army Veterans had very high standards when it came to cleaning. I even explained to him how we spent hours cleaning our weapons. While serving in Iraq, cleaning weapons was a must.

The following night, I went back to the same workstation, but I ended up doing another job, still in the same work section. I had to learn how to put tires on the trailer. I guess the main guy called in sick. Putting tires on trailers was a busting-your-ass kind of job. I didn't mind it at all because I knew working ten hours of doing that would put me to sleep when I got home from work. While doing the tire job, I noticed that the work was aggravating my injuries from war, like my lower back, hips, and knees, but I stuck with the job. I was a little slow at it because I struggled to get the technique down. I figured it was a fast-paced job, as if working at the pit stop for Nascar.

The next night, the main guy started working on installing the tires on the trailer. He was pretty fast and his technique was on point, but he had been doing that job for over a year and he weighed about forty pounds more than me. I spent more days working in that position, and each day I came home tired and in pain. I felt discouraged because I felt like I wasn't making a big impact on working in the tire section. Friday was our overtime day. In fact, all week was overtime (twelve-hour days).

When Friday came around, I thought I would be doing the tire job again, but the supervisor put me back on cleaning panels again. Throughout the night I was getting in trouble for spending too much time cleaning. They wanted me to spot clean and keep moving, which I couldn't do because I could not guarantee that the whole panel walls would get cleaned. The bottom line was I just couldn't do a half-ass job; it's not in my nature.

When the shift was over, I went home and reevaluated my working situation. At this point, I was extremely tired and dirty and my lower back and hips were hurting. I didn't mind going through the pain if it was for the greater good, but at this point it wasn't. It felt like I didn't accomplish a damn thing all week, even though I worked all the overtime they asked of me. I asked myself, *Why did I get this job?* I knew I got this job to pay off some stuff on my credit card and to try to save most of my retirement pay.

The next question that came to mind was, *Who says that you have to clear up your credit really fast?* When that question came up, I realized that I was thinking like a Soldier. In other words, if there is a financial problem, then we, as Soldiers, need to take care of it quickly because it looks bad for the Soldier and the United States Army. But I was not a Soldier anymore, so I decided to quit that job thirty days after being hired. I quit mostly because they never allowed me to work in the sandblasting area, even though I applied for that job and did the interview for that position. By me not doing the job that I applied for, it did nothing but cause aggravated stress on me, which put me in the mind-set that I didn't trust the supervisors. The piss-poor work ethics of young employees was working my last nerve. I worked with young Soldiers of the same age group (eighteen to twenty-four), and they all performed extremely well, especially while in service in Iraq. With that said, Army-trained Soldiers need to maintain a high level of standards for everything we do, and that high level of standards starts on day one in basic training. Now I understand why I don't have the patience to deal with young adult kids who do a half-ass job but expect a full week's pay—even when they miss two days of work.

I had all weekend to decide if I wanted to leave the job. The decision came quickly on Monday morning when I took all my work gear and safety gear to the main office of the company. One of the office workers recognized me and said, "You're terminating your job already?" I told them yes because I had applied for the sandblasting position and ended up working in three other sections. Plus I was beginning to get in trouble for spending too much time cleaning the panel walls, and furthermore, I learned that there was a different type of work ethic between combat Vets and civilians. I told them that I would go back to do what I did best and that was kitchen and bathroom remodeling.

That is where I can maintain my strong work ethic, have complete control of the job, and make a strong impact. Later they asked me how I learned how to do kitchen and bathroom remodels and I told them that I did construction in the Army. When you reach the level of Staff Sergeant (E-6), you need to know all the skill trades (carpentry, masonry, electrical, and plumbing). On top of that, all that you need to know are your construction management skills. With all that said, the people in the office said, "The United States Army has construction?"

I shook my head and said, "You see? That's why I need to quit this job and get back to retirement life." When I turned in everything to them and walked out of the building, I felt so relieved; my headache was gone. I wasn't tense anymore and I felt like I got my personal time back.

As I look back at being an employee there and seeing all the troubles and road blocks that were put in front of me, I believe that was God's way of telling me that I did not belong there; He needed me elsewhere. With that said, He did want me elsewhere because two days later I started a bathroom remodel job.

God Will Put You Where He Needs You to Serve His Children

I got a call from a new customer, another military service member, who needed his bathroom redone. He bought the house in Roy, Utah. I managed to get the bathroom remodel job through my old boss, "Sergeant First Class (E-7)" from Fort Shafter, Hawaii, who was stationed down in Salt Lake City. My boss knew I was retired and lived in Utah. He informed his buddy that I was a retired Construction Engineer and did bathroom and kitchen remodels from time to time. Since my old boss spoke highly of me, when I met the homeowners, they were very happy to meet me. I showed them a fifteen-minute video of construction projects I had done for the Army as well as home remodeling projects. Since they were pleased with my past work history, they allowed me to tackle the bathroom remodel. The bathroom had the 1990s look, which was extremely outdated.

We spent two days or so planning out the bathroom. The wife told me that she wanted to have her bathroom look and feel like the bathroom at a hotel resort establishment that one might see in Hawaii or Guam. With my creative mind-set, I told her, "Not a problem. I will make it happen."

The bathroom projects consisted of tearing out the old bathtub/shower walls. I ended up using my coordinating skills to outsource the job to a company in Sandy to install the bathtub/shower walls. We then planned out the kitchen and bathroom sink design. The old vanity sink base was a single sink, but the bathroom sink base was five feet long. Since the customer wanted a double sink bowl, the kitchen and bath design created a nice bathroom sink base with three drawers in the middle of the wooden cabinet sink base along with open storage space on the left and right. The granite countertop that was for the bathroom sink was also outsourced to have someone do the markup and to make the cut for the faucets and undermount square sinks.

My labor part of the projects consisted of tearing out the bathtub/shower walls, tearing out the old toilet, tearing out cabinet sink base, tearing out floor tiles, making wall repairs, and prepping for painting. I had a three-week turnaround before the bathtub, shower, and wall guys came in to the install. So for three weeks, my job was to paint the ceiling bright white, paint the walls, and install new light fixtures, as well as floors tiles that looked like wood flooring. The tile job took the longest, but the finished work came out great. I used a whole gallon of sealer to seal the floors and conducted a water bead test to see if water would bead up after the tiles were sealed. I allowed the water to stay on the floor for ten minutes; it stayed beaded on top of the tiles and grout lines. In other words, since the sealer sealed the tiles and grout lines, they would never soak up any water. I covered the tile floors with heavy duty pink paper so it wouldn't get dirty while the bath and shower wall guys did the install.

I was able to have a little break. I was done seven days before the bath and shower wall guys came in for install. When the job was complete, the new walls looked like sheets of granite with the bull-nose finished edge and high-gloss finished shine.

During this time, the new resort bathroom was starting to take shape. Our next holdup was waiting for the bathroom sink base. The custom-made wooden double sink base arrived a week and a half after the shower and tub wall guys completed their job. When the vanity base arrived at my favorite hardware store, I didn't know it came in three separate pieces. I delivered the three pieces to the customer's house and began the install.

As I was installing the bathroom vanity sink base, I realized that during the planning stage of the bathroom with the kitchen and design people, I made a special point to order shorter drawers, because I had a feeling that the original size drawers would interfere with the drain line from the back wall of the bathroom. As I suspected, I was glad that I saw the problem that far in advance because the shorter drawers I ordered were two inches short of the drain line. When the three pieces were installed, I immediately made the call for the granite guys to come out and to do measurements for the sizes.

A week later, the granite countertop guys came to do the install. They made the two cutouts for each sink and cut out holes for the two faucets. The bathroom was about 80 percent complete, and the vision of a resort bathroom was coming to life.

The next day, I decided to hook up all the water lines for both sinks. The drain line was not your ordinary installation. The sinks today are deeper than the popular sinks back in the nineties. Now in this particular bathroom, the drain line coming from the wall was much higher than normal, and it made me wonder what the plumber was thinking when the house was built back in then. I noticed from the beginning but I didn't think it would be an issue. However, since the sinks today are deeper and the drain is higher than normal, I had to create a genius way to make the drain system work for both sinks. After all, the water supply lines and drain lines were all connected. I conducted several water tests to check for leaks. Shortly afterward, I conducted the final finishes—towel racks, bathroom door with fresh paint, new door hinges, and doorknob.

When everything was finalized, the homeowners were thrilled with their new bathroom. I was happy to give the homeowners what they wanted. I was also happy that my construction management skills, coordinating skills, and valuable trade skills helped to pull this bathroom together. I was two for two working with homeowners who were service members in our military. I find a great joy in supplying good service and construction/management skills for our service members. The kitchen and bathroom remodels never get old. I hope to be connected to other service members so I can provide them with the quality work, quality customer service, and protect them from shady contractors.

During the six weeks I worked at the house, some of their neighbors saw me as I was got tools out of my truck, but no one stopped to say hello or introduce themselves to me. Most of them would look and keep going as if I did not belong in that neighborhood.

There was this one homeowner six houses down who saw my truck each day, but never saw me. One evening, the homeowner was walking her dog and asking my customer what type of work was being done in her home. My customer said she was getting her bathroom remodeled and that the project was coming along smoothly. The homeowner six houses down wanted to meet me because she was looking to get her bathroom and kitchen done.

When I completed the job and packed all my tools, my customer walked me down to meet the lady. When we approached her doorstep for the meet-and-greet, the homeowners were acting all funny, saying that it was a bad time; she was putting her groceries away and had the dog in the house. Being the way I am, I can read between the lines to know that she would not ever allow a black man in her house, regardless of how good of a job they could do.

As I mentioned earlier, she never saw the color of my skin. She only saw the color of my white truck each day. From what I've seen so far from being at war, it seems like I was good enough to put my life on the line to fight for and protect America's freedom, but I'm not good enough to work in your house to give you the bathroom or kitchen remodel you have always wanted.

I wish in this day in age that we as Americans could put our religious beliefs and the color of our skin aside and work together to achieve a common goal. If the United States Army looked at each Soldier based on skin color and religion, Soldiers would not work well as a team, and a lot of wars would be lost. So open up your minds, people. I believe I would be one of the most trustworthy guys ever to work on your home. I may be retired, but I still carry the seven Army Core Values.

I would truly like to give thanks to my old boss from Hawaii for referring his buddy to me, and I would give thanks to the homeowners for giving me the opportunity to remodel their bathroom. Service members helping out service members—that's how it's done.

Two weeks later, I had to retire Big Hemi after almost two hundred thousand miles. I discovered that it had some bad engine problems, and I had no choice but to look for another truck. I was sad and heartbroken. My hemi and I had some history together, and losing my truck was like losing a battle buddy in the battlefield. On February 21, 2015, I made a point to get a new truck. I knew I had a lot against me, like my credit, but I was working it off steadily with my retirement pay and whatever side jobs I could get. I found a white Dodge 2013 Hemi with only 29,500 miles. Yes, it had all the bells and whistles and then some.

As I look back on how lucky I was to have a new truck with all the bad things on my credit, I have to say it was nothing but an act of God that allowed me to have this truck. Since I have had the truck, I have truly understood what my calling is: continue doing what I do best. I just hope that God will put those who need my skills and services in my path, so I can take care of them.

After working on two service member's houses, I feel a great sense of accomplishment, and I have regained my sense of purpose. I've even regained passion in my dream job that is required for me to buy my own house. I don't know where the money will come from, but my dream job is to buy ten homes, remodel them so I will have something to do during the day, and then rent them out. I believe while having these ten homes, I can also create jobs by having a realtor manage all ten homes and hire my landscaper (fellow Veteran) to cut and trim the yards. I will continue to outsource jobs that I know I can't do, like granite countertops and bath and shower wall installations. I guess I'm just one man who is doing his best to create jobs for small businessmen and my fellow Veterans. I believe creating jobs helps boost the economy, something that our government needs to look into instead of seeking ways to cut Veterans' and fellow service members' benefits.

Learning and Understanding God's Words

During my two side job adventures, I missed a lot of Sundays at church. I didn't feel bad about it because God knows I was out doing His work, though I have to admit that I was missing out on God's words and understanding how His words can add a positive outlook in my life.

I remember when I was eighteen years old, working in the foundry with my dad. When I got laid off, two years later I truly believed that God was speaking to me through my daddy by saying that if I was not planning to go to college, I needed to go somewhere and learn a trade skill. Well, as you can see, I listened. I really mastered my craft, which enabled me to build three buildings in the Marshall Islands, two schools in Thailand, and a floor-laying project in American Samoa, not to mention construction missions all over Iraq and remodels for homes owned by our Veterans and service members while living in Hawaii.

When my hands were free from side jobs, I started attending church, not just on Sundays, but on Wednesday nights as well. I guess you can say my mind was like a sponge ready to absorb God's Word and understand those words. One of the scriptures that I've learned and that fits me very well, since carpentry is my main skill, is from Genesis 6:14: "Make for yourself an ark of gopher wood; you shall make the ark with rooms, and shall cover it inside and out with pitch." At this point in my life, I wish God would send me a message to build an ark, with all the bad things happening in the world, I believe God will do the same thing today as He did back in Noah's days. There are a few other scriptures I've learned that help me deal with life more effectively while I still struggle with PTSD from time to time.

(Proverbs 24:16)

"For a righteous man falls seven times, and rises again, but the wicked stumble in time of calamity."

In my opinion, this scripture tells me that yes I have fallen seven times while having issues from war, but there's another scripture (2 Corinthians 12:10) that I believe supports this quote (Proverbs 24:16).

2 Corinthians 12:10 explains how even though I was weak, I am still strong.

Therefore, I accept weakness, mistreatment, hardship, persecution, and difficulties suffered for Christ. It's clear that when I'm weak, I'm strong. My conclusion is after my fourth tour in Iraq (November 2009), I became weak with the inner demons from war that were getting the very best of me and caused me to feel unsafe in society. However, I fought tooth and nail for three years to get psychiatric treatment from the United States Army.

I'm still receiving treatment, and I have no choice but to move forward and hope that I will see that light at the end of the tunnel. Continuing with the treatment and moving forward is my only option if I want to function in society. So learning that last sentence of that scripture lets me know that yes, I am weak, but I am strong. Thank you, Jesus.

Another scripture I've learned that helps keep my anxiety at bay is Matthew 6:34: "Therefore, stop worrying about tomorrow, because tomorrow will worry about itself. Each day has enough trouble of its own." From this day forward (February 19, 2015), if I can remember this Bible scripture, each day of my retirement life will be easy like Sunday morning. The Holy Bible has many messages that fit in all walks of life. One of the Bible messages that I believe fits for all Veterans who suffer from PTSD after multiple tours in Iraq, Afghanistan, and past wars is Matthew 11:38: "Come to me, all you who are weary and burdened, and I will give you rest." With that said, when I finally retired I saw that I needed to attend church and open my heart and soul to the Lord so He could give me rest. So far, things are going pretty well.

I would like to give thanks to each and every one of you for taking the time to read my book and understand the big picture of the invisible wounds from war. I hope everyone has learned something from the book, and I hope everyone has gained some inspiration. I hope everyone understands the character of Jocephus Josey Duckworth. May God bless you all and let us not forget our fellow service members who fought and died for America's freedom.

Staff Sergeant Duckworth out.

About the Author

Jocephus Josey Duckworth
Facebook: Jocephus Duckworth
Email: duckworthjoe@hotmail.com

- Home Town : Oakland, California
- Meltzer Boys & Girls Club (1984 to 1985).
- Attended Fairfield High school 1986-1990.
- Attended Clearfield Job Corp (January 14,1992 to December 15, 1993)
- Residential Living: G Dorm.
- Trades Completed: (Landscaping & Floor Covering).
- Labor Contribution of Landscaping the Dinosaur Park in Ogden, Utah.

Military History

- Enlisted in The United States Army: November 1996.
- Duty Stations: Fort Wainwright Alaska, Fort Sill Oklahoma, Schofield Barracks, Hawaii.
- Military Occupational Specialty: 12Hotel Construction Supervisor.
- Rank: Staff Sergeant (SSG) Retired E6.

Construction Mission

- 4 Tours to Iraq (January 2003 to November 2009).
- 2 Tours to Marshall Islands (Kwajalien) 1998 & 2000.
- 3 Tours to Thailand (1999 / 2007/2008) Cobra Gold.
- 2 Tours to American Samoa (2011/ 2012).

US Army Awards

- 1 Meritorious Service Medal.
- 3 Army Commendation Medal.
- 5 Army Achievement Medal.
- 1 Combat Action Badge.

Made in the USA
San Bernardino, CA
24 October 2018